Learning to Pass

CLAiT Plus 2006

City College

e-publication design

SOUTHAMPTON
CITY COLLEGE
LEARNING CENTRE

Unit 4

**Penny Hill &
Ruksana Patel**

www.heinemann.co.uk
✓ Free online support
✓ Useful weblinks
✓ 24 hour online ordering

01865 888058

Heinemann

Inspiring generations

Heinemann Educational Publishers
Halley Court, Jordan Hill, Oxford OX2 8EJ
Part of Harcourt Education

Heinemann is the registered trademark of Harcourt Education Limited

Text © Penny Hill and Ruksana Patel, 2006

First published 2006

10 09 08 07 06
10 9 8 7 6 5 4 3 2 1

British Library Cataloguing in Publication Data is available from the British
Library on request.

10-digit ISBN: 0 435 46345 4
13-digit ISBN: 978 0 435 46345 4

Typeset by TechType, Abingdon, Oxon

Original illustrations © Harcourt Education Limited, 2006

Cover design by Wooden Ark

Printed by CPI Bath

Cover photo: © Getty Images

Acknowledgements
The authors would like to thank Stephe and Mur Cove and Rebecca Hill
for working through the book and the tasks and for providing invaluable
feedback. Thank you to Brian Hill, Abdul Patel, Fayaz and Fozia Roked,
for their help, encouragement and support. Thank you to Lewis Birchon
and Gavin Fidler for their invaluable input which has improved the quality
of the book and for their constant support, advice and patience during
the production process. And finally, we would like to thank each other for
"being there for each other".

Contents

The Definition of terms can be found on the CD-ROM that accompanies this book.

Unit 4: e-publication design

This book has been designed to cover the syllabus for Unit 4: e-publication design of the OCR Level 2 Certificate/Diploma for IT Users (CLAiT Plus) and can be used as a basis of learning the skills for the ITQ qualification. Unit 4 is one of seven optional units from the CLAiT Plus qualification.

Learning outcomes for Unit 4: e-publication design

A candidate following a programme of learning leading to this unit will be able to:

- identify and use appropriate software correctly in accordance with laws and guidelines, keeping risks to self and others to a minimum
- use appropriate techniques to handle and organise and save files
- set up and use master page/template according to a design brief
- set up page layout grids/guides
- use most tools and techniques appropriately
- import and manipulate text and image file(s)
- amend publication content using proof correction symbols
- produce professional publications/documents
- prepare a publication for press.

CLAiT Plus

The OCR Level 2 Certificate/Diploma for IT Users (CLAiT Plus) is a qualification designed to recognise the skills, knowledge and understanding of IT users in employment, education or training. It aims to provide a nationally recognised standard in IT assessment that is accessible and flexible whilst also being reliable, consistent and valid. It is designed to fit the needs of the learner, employer and training provider.

The redeveloped qualification

CLAiT Plus has been redeveloped to produce a qualification that provides a clear progression route, from Level 1 to Level 3, at both unit level and whole qualification level. It will equip learners with the range of transferable skills necessary to meet the demands of the modern workplace, and will prepare learners for progression to further training and accreditation in IT User skills at Level 3.

The new qualification maps to the National Occupational Standards for IT Users created by e-skills UK. This takes account of recent software developments and provides greater flexibility, ease-of-use and relevance.

Aims of the qualification

The qualification aims to develop the following:

- knowledge of IT hardware and software and the ability to operate equipment correctly and safely
- knowledge of a range of different software applications and the ability to use different applications effectively to complete complex tasks
- the ability to manage and manipulate complex documents and data in a variety of applications
- the ability to manipulate and integrate data across different applications
- the ability to enter data accurately
- skills and knowledge in contexts that are directly relevant to employment situations
- a natural progression route for candidates who have completed a Level 1 qualification or have basic computer skills.

Structure of the qualification

UNIT STATUS	UNIT TITLE
Core unit	Unit 1: Integrated e-document production
Optional units	Unit 2: Manipulating spreadsheets and graphs
	Unit 3: Creating and using a database
	Unit 4: e-publication design
	Unit 5: Design an e-presentation
	Unit 6: e-image manipulation
	Unit 7: Website creation
	Unit 8: Electronic communication

All units are equally weighted. Candidates may work towards the units in any particular order and learning programmes can be tailored to meet individual needs.

Guided learning hours

An average candidate that has the stated recommended prior learning suggested by OCR should take around 30 guided learning hours per unit to acquire the knowledge, understanding and skills necessary to pass that unit. However, this figure is for guidance only and will vary depending on individual candidates and the mode of learning.

Recommended prior learning

There are no formal requirements for CLAiT Plus, but the CLAiT Plus units assume familiarity with IT concepts at Level 1. There are no minimum entry requirements. However, it is expected that candidates will be working at around Level 2 of the National Qualifications Framework. Candidates will benefit from development of skills assessed through the OCR Level 1 for IT Users (New CLAiT) qualification.

Assessment

Units 1 to 8 are assessed in a centre by a centre assessor and are then externally moderated by an OCR examiner-moderator. OCR sets the assessments, but will allow centres/candidates to produce a suitably appropriate personalised scenario and tasks which allow the candidate to achieve all assessment objectives as listed in individual unit specifications. Candidates are allowed a notional duration of 3 hours for each assessment. If candidates do not pass an OCR-set assignment at the first attempt, they may have other attempts at a unit using a different OCR-set assignment. In order to achieve a unit pass, candidates must make no critical errors and no more than six accuracy errors. For detailed marking criteria please refer to the OCR Level 2 Certificate/Diploma for IT Users (CLAiT Plus) *Tutor's Handbook*.

Alternative forms of assessment

Centres are able to purchase Microsoft Office Specialist tests through OCR and use these as an alternative assessment method towards the following units:

MICROSOFT OFFICE SPECIALIST TEST	OCR UNIT TO BE CLAIMED
Word core	Unit 1: Integrated e-document production
Excel core	Unit 2: Manipulating spreadsheets and graphs
Access core	Unit 3: Creating and using a database
PowerPoint core	Unit 5: Design an e-presentation
Outlook core	Unit 8: Electronic communication

Certification

Candidates may achieve individual unit certificates, an OCR Level 2 Certificate For IT Users (CLAiT Plus) or an OCR Level 2 Diploma For IT Users (CLAiT Plus).

Each unit is regarded as a worthwhile achievement in its own right. Candidates have the option of achieving as many or as few units as are appropriate for their own learning needs or employment situation. Candidates will be awarded a unit certificate for each individual unit achieved.

To achieve the Level 2 Certificate for IT Users qualification, candidates are required to achieve **three** units including the core unit (Unit 1).

Candidates who achieve **five** units, including the core unit (Unit 1), will be awarded an OCR Level 2 Diploma for IT Users.

Progression

Candidates who are successful in achieving accreditation at Level 2 will be able to progress to the OCR Level 3 Certificate/Diploma for IT Users. CLAiT Plus also provides a basis for progression to the NVQs which form part of the ITQ suite, NVQ Levels 1, 2 and 3 for IT Users.

Introduction to ITQ

This book covers the syllabus for Unit 4 of CLAiT Plus. The skills you are learning through this study are important for employment; skills in the use of IT are needed in 9 out of 10 new jobs in the UK. This foreword explains how you can make your study even more valuable. Your successful completion of this CLAiT unit can contribute to achieving an ITQ, and your progress towards an ITQ (including your completion of this CLAiT unit) can be recorded in an e-skills Passport.

The ITQ qualification and e-skills Passport

Both the ITQ and the e-skills Passport have been created by employers. The ITQ is a flexible IT user qualification and training package that can be tailored to ensure you are trained in the IT skills that you need for your job. The ITQ is the new National Vocational Qualification (NVQ) for IT Users. It forms part of the new Apprenticeship Framework for IT Users and is based on the e-skills UK National Occupational Standards.

The e-skills Passport is an online tool that helps you build your IT User skills profile. The e-skills Passport provides a simple means for you to assess the level of your IT skills, plan your ITQ and demonstrate your progress and achievements to date. It is not a qualification, nor is it a formal appraisal system but it is a means to steer you towards the right mix of training and/or qualifications that suit you and your employer. This will give you your personal record of achievement, presented in a form that is widely understand and recognised by employers.

Although the e-skills Passport provides an essential understanding of the IT User skills that you need prior to undertaking ITQ, it is also recommended before embarking on CLAiT Plus 2006. For more information visit the e-skills Passport website (www.e-skillspassport.com).

CLAiT Plus 2006 and the ITQ

CLAiT Plus 2006 units can contribute towards the optional units for the ITQ qualification at Level 2 as shown in the table below. The knowledge, understanding and skills content for CLAiT Plus 2006 units are also based on the National Occupational Standards.

ITQ UNITS	CLAIT PLUS 2006 UNITS
Word processing Level 2 (WP2)	Unit 1: Integrated e-document production
Spreadsheet software Level 2 (SS2)	Unit 2: Manipulating spreadsheets and graphs
Database software Level 2 (DB2)	Unit 3: Creating and using a database
E-mail Level 2 (MAIL2)	Unit 8: Electronic communication
Presentation software Level 2 (PS2)	Unit 5: Design an e-presentation
Website software Level 2 (WEB2)	Unit 7: Website creation
Artwork and imaging software Level 2 (ART2)	Unit 6: e-image manipulation

The ITQ calculator

The ITQ can be achieved at three levels. Each component unit at each level has been allocated a number of points. The tables below also show the total number of points that need to be achieved for ITQ at each level. You can select units from different levels in order to achieve the desired number of points, provided you take the mandatory unit (Make selective use of IT) and at least 60% of your unit choices are at the ITQ level that you wish to achieve.

	ITQ LEVELS		
	Level 1	Level 2	Level 3
Total required	40	100	180
Total of points to come from optional units at level of qualification	15	40	75

For example, for a Level 2 qualification:

- overall points total of 100
- 25 points come from mandatory unit
- 75 points come from optional units
- of the 75 optional points 40 must be achieved at Level 2.

ITQ internal credit matrix

UNIT TITLES	UNIT VALUES		
	Level 1	Level 2	Level 3
Mandatory unit			
Make selective use of IT	15	25	35
Optional units			
Using IT systems	5	15	25
Operate a computer	10	20	30
IT troubleshooting for users	5	15	25
IT maintenance for users	5	15	25
IT security for users	5	15	25
Use IT to exchange information	5	15	25
Internets and intranets	5	15	25
E-mail	5	15	25
Word processing	10	20	30
Spreadsheets	10	20	35
Databases	10	20	35
Websites	10	20	35
IT artwork and images	10	20	35
IT presentations	10	20	30
Specialist or bespoke software	10	20	30
Evaluate the impact of IT	5	15	25
Sector specific unit	10	20	30

For more information about ITQ, visit the ITQ website (www.ITQ.org.uk).

Who this book is suitable for

This book is suitable for:

- candidates working towards:
  - OCR Level 2 Certificate/Diploma for IT Users (CLAiT Plus)
  - OCR ITQ qualification
- use as a self-study workbook – the user should work through the book from start to finish
- tutor-assisted workshops or tutor-led groups
- individuals wishing to extend their skills in Microsoft Office Publisher 2003 (default settings are assumed).

Although this book is based on Publisher 2003, it may also be suitable for users of Microsoft Publisher 2002 (XP). Note that some features will be different and some screenshots will not be identical.

UNIT 4: e-publication design

How to use this book

This book is written for one unit of the syllabus. Separate books are available for each of the other units. A compendium book containing units 1, 2 and 3 is also available.

In Unit 4: e-publication design, you will need to follow a design brief to create a range of publications/documents, using standard and non-standard page sizes, create a template and use this to create several publications. Import and manipulate text and graphics, use checking, proof-correction and copyfitting techniques, and prepare publications for press.

This book is divided into five sections:

- in Section 1, you will learn how to create a master page and templates
- in Section 2, you will learn how to use design briefs, layout diagrams and text flow diagrams to display page content
- in Section 3, you will learn how to create and use style sheets and correct text according to proof correction symbols
- in Section 4, you will learn how to create special text effects, format objects and produce a variety of publications
- in Section 5, you will learn how to copyfit and print templates and publications.

You will use a software program called Microsoft Office Publisher 2003 which is part of Microsoft Office 2003. Publisher is a desktop publishing program which allows you to combine text and graphics to create professional publications with relative ease. We will refer to it as Publisher from now on. Default settings in Publisher are assumed.

How to work through this book

This book assumes knowledge of Level 1 skills in using Publisher to create a single-page publication combining text and images, and Level 1 desktop publishing terms.

1 Read the explanation of a term first.

2 If there are some terms you do not understand, refer to the **Definition of terms** on the CD-ROM.

3 Work through the book in sequence so that one skill is understood before moving on to the next. This ensures understanding of the topic and prevents unnecessary mistakes.

4 Read the **▶▶ How to...** guidelines which give step-by-step instructions for each skill. Do not attempt to work through the How to… guidelines, but read through each point and look at the screenshots. Make sure that you understand all the instructions before moving on.

5 To make sure that you have understood how to perform a skill, work through the **Check your understanding** task following that skill. You should refer to the How to… guidelines when doing the task.

6 At the end of each section is an **Assess your skills** list. Read through these lists to find out how confident you feel about the skills that you have learned.

7 Towards the end of the book are **Quick reference guides, Build-up** and **Practice tasks**. Work through each of the tasks.

8 If you need help, you may refer to the How to… guidelines or Quick reference guides while doing the Build-up tasks. Whilst working on the Practice tasks, you should feel confident enough to use only the Quick reference guides if you need support. These guides may also be used during an assessment.

A CD-ROM accompanies this book. On it are the files that you will need to use for the tasks. Instructions for copying the files are given below. The solutions for all the tasks can be found on the CD-ROM in a folder called **L2U4EDP_worked.**

Note: there are many ways of performing the skills covered in this book. This book provides How to… guidelines that have proven to be easily understood by learners.

Files for this book

To work through the tasks in this book, you will need the files from the folder called **L2U4EDP_files.** This folder is on the CD-ROM provided with this book. Copy this folder into your user area before you begin.

To practise a particular skill you may use the files provided in the L2U4EDP_worked folder.

▶▶ How to... *copy the folder L2U4EDP_files from the CD-ROM*

1 Insert the CD-ROM into the CD-ROM drive of your computer.

2 Close any windows that may open.

3 From the desktop, double-click the **My Computer** icon to display the **My Computer** window.

4 Double-click on the **CD drive** icon.

5   A dialogue box will open displaying the contents of the CD-ROM. Click once on the folder **L2U4EDP_files**. The folder will be highlighted (usually blue).

6   In the **File and Folder Tasks** section, click on **Copy this folder**.

7   The **Copy Items** dialogue box will be displayed. In this dialogue box, click on the user area where you want to copy the folder **L2U4EDP_ files** to.

8   Click on the **Copy** button. The folder **L2U4EDP_files** will be copied to your user area.

TIP!

It is advisable to copy and paste a second copy to another folder in your user area as backup.

Preparing your work area

You are advised to prepare your user area to keep your files organised.

○ Create a folder for your CLAiT Plus work.

○ In this folder, create a subfolder for all the CLAiT Plus units that you will be doing.

○ In each unit subfolder, create further subfolders, for example:

 • **U4EDP working**:   your working folder in which all working files will be saved.

 • **L2U4EDP_files**:   the source files folder copied from the CD-ROM.

 • **L2U4EDP_worked**: the worked copies folder also copied from the CD-ROM.

Terms and symbols used in this book

Unless otherwise instructed, always click using the left mouse button.

TERM	ACTION
Click	Press and release the *left* mouse button once
Double-click	Quickly press the left mouse button *twice* then release it
Right-click	Press the *right* mouse button once
Drag	Press and hold down the left mouse button while moving the mouse
Select	Click on an item or highlight text
Hover	Position the mouse pointer over an icon or menu item and pause. A Tool tip or a further menu item will appear
+ (e.g. Ctrl + P)	Used to indicate that two keys should be held down together
→	Indicates a new instruction follows

In this section you will learn how to:

- ⊙ work with Master Pages and templates
- ⊙ use the zoom tools
- ⊙ display the Master Page
- ⊙ create a non-standard page
- ⊙ save a publication
- ⊙ set margin and column guides
- ⊙ insert headers and footers.

Working with Publisher

When working with Publisher you will need to place items precisely on the page. It is therefore helpful to have as much of the page visible on the screen as possible. Closing the task pane will create a larger working area for your publications. You can display the task pane at any point when you are working with a publication.

You can close the task pane when you load the program and at any point when you are working with the publication.

When you start Publisher a new blank publication will open automatically.

▶▶ How to... *close the task pane and start a new publication*

1   Load Publisher.

2   Click the ✕ (Figure 4.1).

3   The task pane and the opening screen will close and a blank publication will be opened.

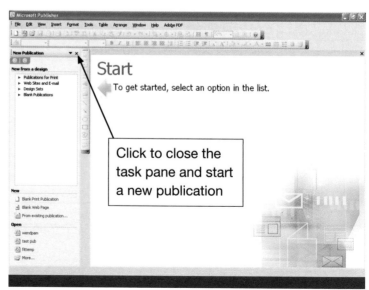

Click to close the task pane and start a new publication

FIGURE 4.1 Closing the task pane after loading Publisher

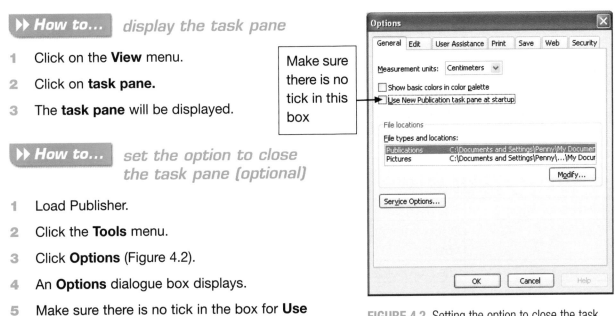

►► How to... *display the task pane*

1 Click on the **View** menu.

2 Click on **task pane.**

3 The **task pane** will be displayed.

►► How to... *set the option to close the task pane (optional)*

1 Load Publisher.

2 Click the **Tools** menu.

3 Click **Options** (Figure 4.2).

4 An **Options** dialogue box displays.

5 Make sure there is no tick in the box for **Use New Publication task pane at startup**.

Make sure there is no tick in this box

FIGURE 4.2 Setting the option to close the task pane

Getting familiar with the Publisher window

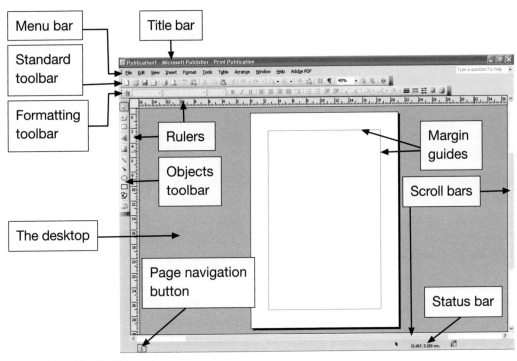

Menu bar

Title bar

Standard toolbar

Formatting toolbar

Rulers

Objects toolbar

Margin guides

Scroll bars

The desktop

Page navigation button

Status bar

FIGURE 4.3 The Publisher window

Take a few minutes to become familiar with the different parts of Publisher.

Title bar	Displays the name of the current publication *(Publication1), the name of the program (Microsoft Publisher) and the type of publication (print publication).
Menu bar	A list of options. Click on a menu item to see the drop-down menu.
Standard toolbar	Includes icons for commonly used tasks, e.g. save, print, etc.
Formatting toolbar	Includes icons commonly used for formatting text, e.g. bold, centre. The icons are ghosted (pale grey) if the publication is blank or if a text box is not selected.
Objects toolbar	Displays icons used to create objects on a page, e.g. text box, picture frame, etc.
Blank publication	The main publication in the centre of the screen.
Status bar	Displays the number of pages in a publication and the position and size of objects.
Margin guide	The blue borders within the publication.
Rulers	Horizontal and vertical rulers are displayed. Rulers help position objects accurately in a publication.
Page navigation button	Displays the current page number [1] (Figure 4.3) in the publication or displays as [A] in Master Page view.

Understanding Master Pages and templates

A template is set up to assist in creating a consistent appearance across all pages in a publication (or a series of publications). In Publisher the **Master Page** can be used to create a template to display the design and layout elements that are to be repeated on multiple pages in a publication. Amendments to these elements can then be made on the Master Page, rather than making them on each page of the publication.

The page orientation, margins, number of columns and space between columns can be set on the Master Page. In Publisher setting these items on the Master Page places guides on each page of the publication. These guides will assist in placing items consistently and accurately throughout the publication. In Publisher page items can be placed outside the layout guides.

Objects that are to appear in precisely the same position on every page should be placed on the Master Page (e.g. a company logo, the name of the publication, chapter name and/or number). Items that are placed on the Master Page will appear in exactly the same position on every page of the publication and cannot accidentally be moved when working on individual pages.

When working on individual pages it is possible to place items (e.g. text and graphics) outside of the Master Page guides. However, items that have been placed on the Master Page cannot be moved when working on the individual pages. It is possible to hide the master items on any individual page, but they can only be repositioned or amended by adjusting them on the Master Page.

TIP!

Margins and columns in Publisher are only position guides – items can still be placed outside the page margins.

The zoom tools

Desktop published documents often require fine detail and precise positioning. The zoom tools on the **Standard Toolbar** allow you to enlarge particular parts of the page (zoom in) so that you can work more closely with particular items. You may also want to reduce the view of the page so that you can see the page as a whole (zoom out).

To zoom in or out either use the drop-down zoom menu (Figure 4.4), or the **Zoom In** 🔍 or **Zoom Out** 🔍 icon.

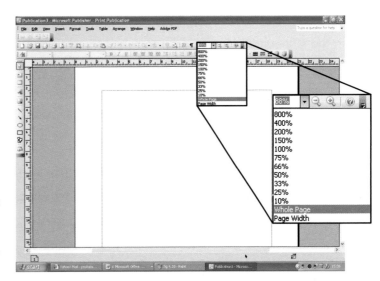

FIGURE 4.4 The zoom menu

TIP!

If you close a file whilst in Master Page view, it may not re-open in Master Page view To work in Master Page view, you must remember to display the Master Page again.

▶▶ How to... *display the Master Page*

1   Click on the **View** menu.

2   Click on **Master Page**.

3   The Master Page will display and an **Edit Master Page Task Pane** will display on the screen.

4   The Page Navigation button to the left of the status bar displays as [A📄] when the Master Page is displayed.

5   To keep your screen clear, close the **Edit Master Pages** task pane.

▶▶ How to... *create a non-standard page*

1   From **Normal** or **Master Page** view click on the **File** menu.

2   Click on **Page Setup.**

3   The Page Setup dialogue box will display. Click on the **Layout** tab.

4   In the Publication type section click on **Custom**.

5   In the box next to **Width**, enter the required page width.

Click on Custom

Enter page width and height

Select orientation

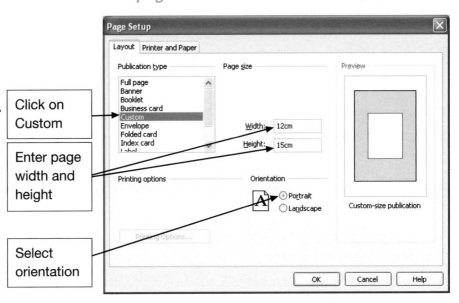

FIGURE 4.5 The Page Setup menu

6   In the box next to **Height**, enter the required page height.

7   In the Orientation section click to select **Portrait** or **Landscape**.

8   Click on **OK**.

▶▶ How to... *save a publication*

1   Click on the **File** menu.

2   Click **Save As**. The **Save As** dialogue box displays.

3   Click on the drop-down arrow to the right of the **Save in** box.

4   Locate your user area and open your working folder.

5   In the **File name** box, delete any existing text and enter the required filename.

6   In the **Save as type** box, make sure **Publisher Files** is displayed.

7   Click the **Save** button.

Check your understanding *Create and save a non-standard* Master Page

1   Load Publisher.

2   Display the Master Page.

3   Close the task pane.

4   Set the page size to:

   Width: 12 cm
   Height 15 cm

5   Set the orientation to **Portrait**.

6   Save the publication as **smallpub**.

▶▶ How to... *set margin and column guides*

1   From the **Master Page** view, click on the **Arrange** menu.

2   Click on **Layout Guides**.

3   A Layout Guides dialogue box displays.

4   In the **Margin Guides** section, enter the measurements for each of the margins.

5   Click on the **Grid Guides** tab.

6   In the **Columns** box, enter the number of columns.

7   Click in the **Preview pane**.

8   In the **Spacing** box enter the space between columns.

9   Click on **OK**.

TIP!

Ensure that there is **no** tick in the box next to the Two-page master, otherwise you may create the wrong master page.

TIP!

If you use the arrows to select the number of columns you do not need to click in the Preview pane.

8   Unit 4: e-publication design

1   Continue working in the publication **smallpub**.

2   Display the Master Page.

3   Set the margins to be 1 cm (10 mm) all round. Do not set any column guides.

4   Save the publication keeping the filename **smallpub**.

5   From the **File** menu, close the publication.

6   Create a new publication.

7   In the new publication display the Master Page.

8   Select a full page (A4) in landscape orientation.

9   Set the page layout to be:

Margins	
Left	2 cm (20 mm)
Right	2 cm (20 mm)
Top	3 cm (30 mm)
Bottom	3 cm (30 mm)
Number of columns	3
Space between columns	1 cm (10 mm)

10 Save the publication using the filename **guides**

11 Close the publication.

> **TIP!**
>
> Use the **File** menu to close the publication. If you use the close icon you will close the program not just the publication.

Headers and footers

Headers and footers are generally inserted on the Master Page so that they will appear on every page of the publication.

Publisher places headers and footers in a text box very close to the margin guides of the publication. The header and footer text boxes have internal margins, meaning the text will not align exactly to the left or right margin guides in the publication. Although these text boxes can be moved, it is normally sufficient to remove the internal margins. To create a greater distance from the page content, header text can be aligned to the top of the header text box, and footer text to the bottom of the footer text box. Headers and footers can be aligned to the left, centre or right by clicking on the alignment icons on the standard toolbar.

In Publisher page numbers, the date and the time can be entered automatically by clicking on an icon in the Header and Footer toolbar. When automatic page numbers are inserted on

ICON	FUNCTION
#	Inserts page numbers
🗓	Inserts the date
🕐	Inserts the time

AutoText icons in the Header and Footer toolbar

the Master Page a # sign will appear to show that the correct page number will be shown on each page.

To display several header/footer items on one line press the **Tab** key.

▶▶ How to... *insert headers and footers*

1 Go to Master Page view, click on the **View** menu.

2 Click on **Header and Footer**.

3 A **Header and Footer** toolbar will display.

4 On the Header and Footer toolbar, click on the **Show Header/Footer** icon ⯐ to switch between the header and footer.

5 Click on the **Format** menu.

6 Click on **Text Box**.

7 Click on the **Text Box** tab.

8 In the **Text Box Margin** section set **all** margins to 0.

9 For headers set the **Vertical alignment** to Top.

10 For footers set the **Vertical alignment** to Bottom.

11 Click **OK**.

12 On the Standard toolbar click on the appropriate alignment icon and/ or if required use the **Tab** key to select centre or right alignment.

13 Enter the text and/or click on:

⯐ **Insert Page Number** icon to enter page numbers

⯐ **Insert Date** icon to enter the date

⯐ **Insert Time** icon to enter the time.

14 On the Header and Footer toolbar click on Close .

1 Open the publication **smallpub**.
2 Display the Master Page.
3 Set the internal margins of the header to be 0 cm all round.
4 Set the vertical alignment of the header to top.
5 Insert your name and centre number as a left-aligned header.
6 Save the publication keeping the filename **smallpub**.
7 Close the publication.
8 Open the publication **guides**.
9 Display the Master Page.
10 Insert the following headers and footers:

What does it mean?

Flush
Aligned exactly.

	TEXT	SPACING
Header	Building solutions	Flush to right margin
Footer	Your name, centre number page number	Flush to left margin Centre

Remember to format the text box margins to 0 cm all round and the alignment to top for headers and bottom for footers.

11 Save the publication as **headfoot**
12 Close the publication.

ASSESS YOUR SKILLS – Create a Master Page and template

By working through Section 1 you will have learnt how to:

○ work with Master Pages and templates

○ use the zoom tools

○ display the Master Page

○ create a non-standard page

○ save a publication

○ set margin and column guides

○ insert headers and footers.

If you think that you need more practice on any of the skills in the above list, go back and work through those skills again.

If you feel confident move on to Section 2.

LEARNING OUTCOMES

In this section you will learn how to:

- ○ work with design briefs and page layout guides
- ○ position ruler guides
- ○ remove ruler guides
- ○ import (insert) an image
- ○ resize an image while maintaining proportion
- ○ resize an image to an exact size
- ○ move images
- ○ layer images
- ○ work with text flow diagrams
- ○ insert text
- ○ turn off hyphenation
- ○ create text boxes
- ○ insert pages
- ○ delete pages
- ○ import (insert) a text file and control text flow.

Design briefs and page layout guides

Design briefs give information about the design of a publication, for example, all images must be surrounded by a box. Page layout guides are given to show the approximate position of items that are to be included on the page. How much information is included in the design brief and the page layout sketches, and how they are displayed will depend on the style used by the publishing house or designer. Examples similar to the layout diagrams that you will need to follow are given below.

The following diagram shows the non-printing items of a two-column publication.

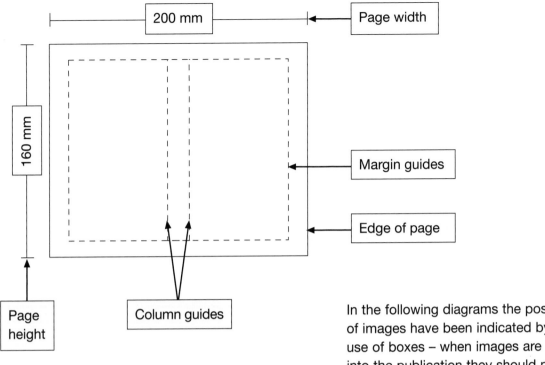

FIGURE 4.6 Non-printing items in a two-column publication

In the following diagrams the positions of images have been indicated by the use of boxes – when images are inserted into the publication they should not be framed by a box unless there is a specific instruction to do so.

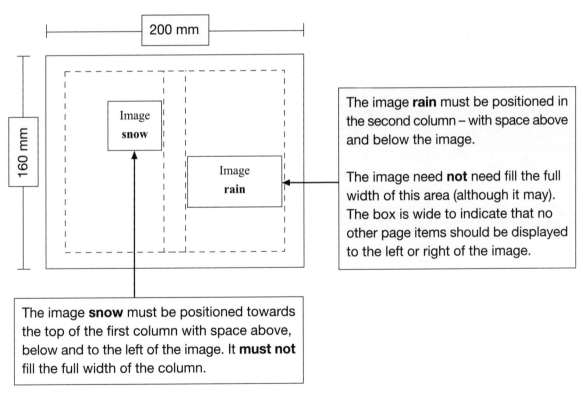

The image **rain** must be positioned in the second column – with space above and below the image.

The image need **not** need fill the full width of this area (although it may). The box is wide to indicate that no other page items should be displayed to the left or right of the image.

The image **snow** must be positioned towards the top of the first column with space above, below and to the left of the image. It **must not** fill the full width of the column.

FIGURE 4.7 Positioning of images

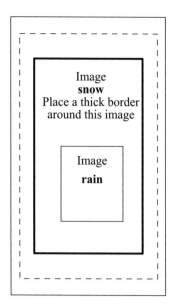

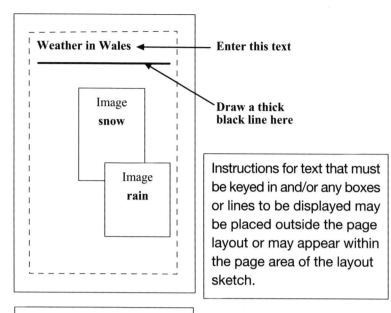

Image **rain** on top of image **snow**
Image **snow** framed by a border

image **rain** partially overlapping image **snow**

Instructions for text that must be keyed in and/or any boxes or lines to be displayed may be placed outside the page layout or may appear within the page area of the layout sketch.

FIGURE 4.8 Overlapping images

Ruler guides

Ruler guides can be used to assist in placing page items accurately. Ruler guides do not print but are shown in green on the page (Figure 4.9).

Position the mouse pointer on the ruler (top ruler for horizontal rulers, left ruler for vertical rulers). The mouse pointer changes to ⬍. Click and drag the ruler to the required position

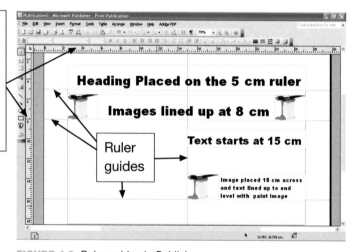

FIGURE 4.9 Ruler guides in Publisher

▶▶ How to... *position ruler guides*

1   Position the mouse on the ruler (top ruler for horizontal guide, left ruler for vertical guide).

2 Click and drag the ruler guide to the required position (use the rulers at the top and side of the page to help you).

3 Release the mouse button.

▶▶ How to... *remove ruler guides*

1 Position the mouse on the ruler guide *in the margin area* of the publication.

2 Click and drag the ruler guide off the page.

3 Release the mouse button. The ruler guide will be removed.

▶▶ How to... *import (insert) an image*

1 On the **Objects** toolbar click on the **Picture Frame** icon 🖼 to display the picture menu.

2 Click on **Picture from File**.

3 The mouse pointer changes to a cross **✛**.

4 Move the mouse to the position in the publication where the image is to be placed.

5 Click and drag to draw a frame approximately the required size.

6 Release the mouse button.

7 An **Insert Picture** dialogue box displays immediately.

8 Locate the image file to be inserted.

9 In the **Files of type** box, make sure that **All Pictures** is displayed.

10 In the main window, click on the image to be inserted.

11 Click **Insert**.

12 The image will be inserted into the picture frame in your publication.

▶▶ How to... *resize an image while maintaining its proportion*

1 Position your mouse on a *corner* handle of the image.

2 The mouse changes to a diagonal arrow ↘ ↙.

3 Click and drag the diagonal arrow inwards to make the image smaller OR outwards to increase its size.

4 Release the mouse button.

What does it mean?

Importing
Placing an image file in a publication is generally referred to as 'importing'. In Publisher this is referred to as 'inserting'.

TIP!

When the image is inserted into the frame the size of the frame will adjust to keep the image in proportion.

TIP!

NEVER resize an image from any of the centre handles (with a straight arrow ↕ or ↔) or the image will become distorted!

How to... *resize an image to an exact size*

1 Right-click on the image.

2 A menu displays.

3 Click on **Format Picture.**

4 A **Format Picture** dialogue box displays.

5 Select the **Size** tab.

6 Check that there are ticks in the boxes for **Lock aspect ratio** and the **Relative to original picture size.**

7 In the **Height** *or* **Width** box enter the required measurement (you cannot enter both or your picture will not be in proportion).

8 Click **OK.**

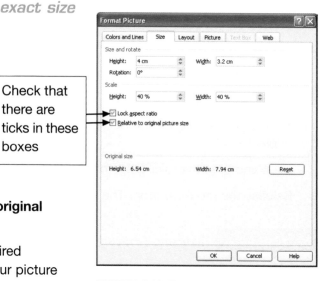

> Check that there are ticks in these boxes

FIGURE 4.10 Resizing images

How to... *move images*

1 Position your mouse on the image.

2 The mouse changes to ✛ (four-headed arrow).

3 Click and drag the image to the required position. Hold down the **Alt** key whilst dragging the image to give you more precise control.

4 Release the mouse button.

Do NOT drag on any of the corner or side handles of the image, or you will distort (change the proportions of) the original image.

TIP!

Make sure you do not have a two-way arrow as this will change the size and/or proportion of the image.

How to... *layer images*

1 Click on image to be layered, round handles will appear around the edge of the image.

2 Right-click on the image.

3 Click on **Order**.

4 From the drop-down menu click on the required option.

TIP!

Images can be layered on other images or on text.

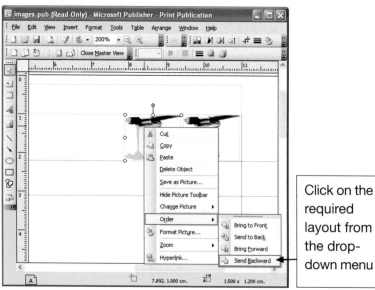

> Click on the required layout from the drop-down menu

FIGURE 4.11 Layering images

1 Open the publication **smallpub**.

2 All items must be placed on the Master Page.

3 Refer to the page layout sketch below when completing all instructions.

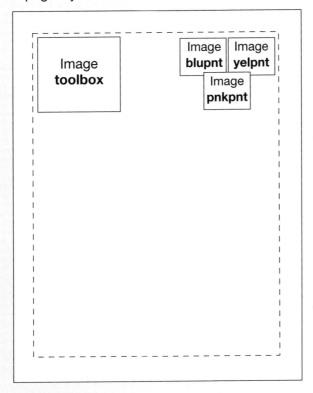

FIGURE 4.12 Page layout sketch

4 All images must be placed in the approximate position shown.

5 Images may be resized, but must be kept in proportion.

6 Make sure that the Master Page is displayed.

7 Import the image **Toolbox** and position it in the top left of the publication.

8 Position a ruler at the bottom of the **Toolbox** image.

9 Import the image **yelpnt** and position it in the top right of the publication.

10 Make sure that the image does not touch or overlap any page items.

11 Import the image **blupnt** and position it to the right of the image **yelpnt**.

12 Make sure that the image does not touch or overlap any page items.

13 Import the image **pnkpnt** and position it so that the bottom of the **pnkpnt** image aligns with the **toolbox** image and the top overlaps the bottom of the **blupnt** and **yelpnt** images.

14 Save the publication as **images**.

15 Close the publication.

Text flow diagrams

Text flow is indicated by lines on the page layout sketch. The start position of the text is generally shown by a straight vertical at the start of the text flow lines |—— the name of the text file that is to be displayed is generally shown under this line. Where the text should end is indicated by a vertical line at the end of the text flow lines ——|. Although the end marker will normally be positioned at the far right of a column the last line of text need not flow up to the right edge of the column, even when the text is justified.

Look at the text flow in the page layout sketch shown below.

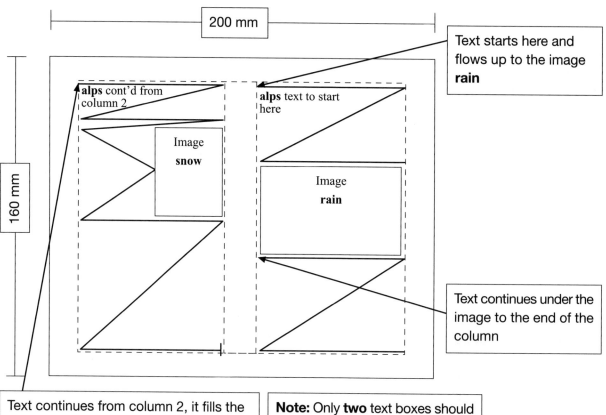

Text starts here and flows up to the image **rain**

alps cont'd from column 2

alps text to start here

Image **snow**

Image **rain**

Text continues under the image to the end of the column

Text continues from column 2, it fills the column above the **snow** image, it continues on the left side of the page up to the image (but not on top or behind it) and then continues under the image filling the width of the column and ending at the margin guide at the end of the page.

Note: Only **two** text boxes should be drawn for the layout of this publication; one for the **entire** 1st column and one for the **entire** 2nd column. The text flow around the images will be controlled by using text wrap.

FIGURE 4.13 Page layout sketch

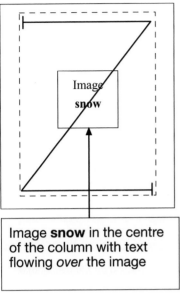

Layering of images and/or text may also be indicated in the layout sketch. Look at the example below:

Image **snow** in the centre of the column with text flowing *over* the image

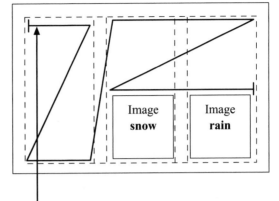

Text may flow across two or more columns. Look at the example below:

Image **snow**

Image **rain**

Text begins at the top of column 1, it fills column 1 and then flows across columns 2 and 3 ending half way down the page. Image **snow** is placed in column 2 and image **rain** in column 3.

FIGURE 4.14 Image layering and text overflow in page layout sketches

Inserting text

In Publisher, text can only be entered or inserted from another file into a text box; text cannot be entered or inserted directly on to a publication page. To control text flow you will need to create individual text boxes for all areas of the publication that are to contain text (not one text box covering the whole page).

To ensure that the text will fill the area of the text box, the internal margins of the text box will need to be set to 0 cm. When importing (inserting) a text file that is to flow into several areas/columns of the publication all the text boxes should be drawn *before* the text file is imported.

When drawing a text box it must be aligned exactly to the page layout guides (e.g. margin and column guides). If the text box is aligned exactly to the guides, then the frame of the box will conceal them (i.e. the blue and/or green guides will not be visible).

Text boxes for text that is to be displayed on all pages of the publication (e.g. the company name) can be created on the Master Page or for text that will be different on each page (e.g. the text of an article) on the individual publication page(s).

TIP!

Text boxes are often referred to as text frames.

You will be required to turn hyphenation off. Although you can do this once the text has been imported or inserted it is quicker and easier to turn the hyphenation off for all text boxes in the publication before any text boxes have been drawn.

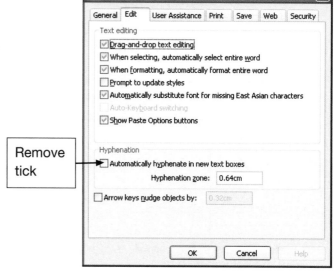

▶▶ How to... *turn off hyphenation*

1   Click on the **Tools** menu.

2   Select **Options**.

3   The Options dialogue box will display. Click on the **Edit** tab (Figure 4.15).

4   In the box next to **Automatically hyphenate in new text boxes**, click to *remove* the tick.

5   Click on **OK**.

▶▶ How to... *create a text box*

FIGURE 4.15 Turning off the hyphenation

1   From the **Objects Toolbar** click the **Text Box** icon ▣.

2   Move the mouse to the position on the page that the text box is to start, the mouse pointer will show as a cross ✛.

3   Click and drag to draw a text box to the required size.

4   Release the mouse button.

5   The text box should display on the page with round handles.

6   Zoom into the page to check that the text box is lined up correctly with the page layout guides.

7   If required, use the handles of the text box to adjust the frame to exactly fit the page layout guides.

*After drawing the **first** text box in a publication:*

8   Ensure the text box is selected.

9   Click on the **Format** menu.

10 Click on **Text Box.**

11 Click on the **Text Box** tab.

12 Set the **Vertical Alignment** (usually Top).

13 Set **Text Box Margins** to 0 cm all round.

14 Check that Text autofitting is set to **Do not autofit.**

15 Click on the **Colors and Lines** tab.

16 Click **Apply settings to new text boxes**.

17 Click on **OK**.

TIP!

If the text box is to be framed with a border, the text box margins will need to be re-set (margins of 0.1 cm all round are normally sufficient) to prevent the text from touching the frame of the box.

1 Open the publication **headfoot**.

2 Refer to the page layout sketch below when following all instructions.

Page 1

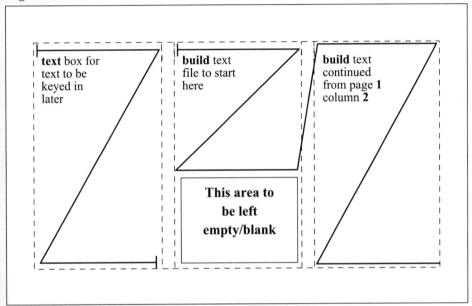

FIGURE 4.16 Page layout sketch

3 Ensure that you are working on page 1 of the publication.

4 Draw a text box to fill the entire first column.

5 Set the text properties (remember to apply settings to new text boxes).

6 In the second column draw a text box to fill just over half of the column.

7 Draw a text box to fill the entire third column.

8 Make sure that all columns are aligned to the appropriate margin and column guides.

9 Save the publication using the filename **p1layout**

10 Close the publication.

Inserting pages

You will need to create a publication consisting of more than one page. Publisher gives you the option to insert either new blank pages or new pages with objects (e.g. text boxes) in the same position as they are on the existing page.

If the publication requires the text flow to be similar on each of the pages (e.g. the text flows into all columns on all pages), you should create the text boxes on the first page and then select the option to insert new pages with duplicate objects. If required, minor amendments to the text boxes can be made on individual pages.

If the layout for each page is very different you can choose to insert blank pages and insert the items for each page individually.

▶▶ How to... *insert pages*

1   Make sure either the page before, or the page after, where the new page is to be inserted is displayed on the screen.

2   Click on the **Insert** menu.

3   Click on **Page**.

4   In the box next to **Number of new pages** enter the number of pages to be inserted. An **Insert Page** dialogue box displays.

5   Click to select **Before current page** or **After current page**.

   *To insert pages with text boxes in the **same** position:*
   ○   Click in **Duplicate all objects on page**.

   ○   Click on **OK**.

   *To insert **empty** pages:*
   ○   Follow steps 1 to 5.

   ○   Click on **Insert blank page**.

   ○   Click on **OK**.

   ○   Use the Page Navigation Buttons [1] [2] to move between the pages.

▶▶ How to... *delete pages*

1   Ensure the page that is to be deleted is displayed on the screen.

2   Click on the **Edit** menu.

3   Click on **Delete page**.

4   The page will be deleted and all pages in the publication will be renumbered to reflect the deletion.

1 Open the publication **p1layout**.

2 Ensure that page 1 of the publication is displayed on the screen.

3 Insert a new **blank** page after page 1 (all the blue guides should be clearly visible on page 2).

4 Use the navigation buttons to move to page 1 (notice how some of the guides are hidden by the frames of the text boxes on page 1).

5 Move back to page 2.

6 Delete page 2. Page 1 should now be visible on the screen.

7 Insert a new page after page 1 ensuring that the new page will have text boxes in the same place as they are on page 1.

8 Use the Page Navigation Buttons to move back to page 1.

9 Save the publication using the filename **twopages**

10 Do not close the publication.

TIP!

Remember: if you make a mistake you can click on the **Undo** icon.

1 Continue working in the publication **twopages**.

2 Refer to Page 2 Layout Sketch when following all instructions.

Page 2

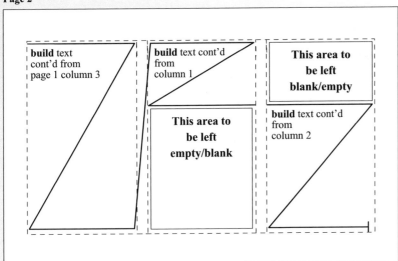

build text cont'd from page 1 column 3

build text cont'd from column 1

This area to be left blank/empty

This area to be left empty/blank

build text cont'd from column 2

FIGURE 4.17 Page 2 Layout Sketch

3 Ensure that you are working on **page 2** of the publication.

4 Adjust the text box in the second column so that it is slightly shorter.

5 Adjust the text box in the third column so that it starts further down the column.

6 Display page 1 on the screen.

7 Save the publication using the filename **textflow**

8 Close the publication.

Importing a text file

When working in publishing it is usually more efficient for the text to be prepared in a word processing package and then imported into the desktop publishing package. The text files are often long and it is very important to ensure that all the text has been imported. You are therefore advised to print the text file before you import it into the publication. This will make it easier for you to check that the entire text file has been imported and is displayed in the publication.

In some publications text does not flow from one column (or page) to the next. For example, text may not start in column 1 of page 1 or some columns (or parts of columns) may contain a different text file. You may find it useful to look at a newspaper to see how some stories are displayed in different columns and sometimes start on one page and finish on another.

When you import a text file it is possible to allow Publisher to flow the text for you. This is useful for long publications, where the text flows from one text box to the next (although you can choose to skip text boxes). However, this method will not be suitable for all publications. You will learn how to flow the text yourself. You will need to use the Connect Text Boxes Toolbar to do this.

In Publisher importing text is referred to as 'inserting' text and the options to insert a text file will be found in the **Insert** menu.

TIP!

Print the text file before importing it into a publication.

▶▶ How to...   *import (insert) a text file and control text flow*

1. Click in the text box where the text is to start (round handles display and a cursor will be flashing in the top left of the text box).

2. Click on the **Insert** menu.

3. Click on **Text File**.

4. An **Insert Text** dialogue box will open.

5. Locate the file to be inserted.

6. In the **Files of type** box, check that **All Text Formats** is displayed.

7. Click on the file to be inserted, then click **OK**.

8. A **File Conversion** dialogue box *may* display, if it does, check that the button for Windows (Default) is selected, then click **OK**.

9. If the text does not fit in the text box the Text Flow dialogue box will appear (Figure 4.18).

10. Click on **No.**

FIGURE 4.18 Controlling text flow

11. The text in overflow symbol **A····** will be displayed at the bottom of the first text box.

12. Click on the **A····** symbol.

TIP!

If the **Connect Text Boxes** toolbox is not displayed click on the **View** menu ➔ **Toolbars** ➔ **Connect Text Boxes**.

13 On the Connect Text Boxes toolbar click on .

14 Move your mouse into the text box where you wish the text to continue (the cursor will have changed to a pouring jug).

15 Check that this is the correct text box then click. The text will flow into the selected text box.

16 Repeat steps 12 to 15 until all the text has been imported.

TIP!

Don't worry if the text does not fill all the text boxes – when you format the publication your text may be larger and you can then continue flowing the text into the remaining text boxes.

Check your understanding *Importing a text file and controlling text flow*

1 Open the publication **text flow**.

2 Refer to the page layout sketch when following all instructions.

Page 1

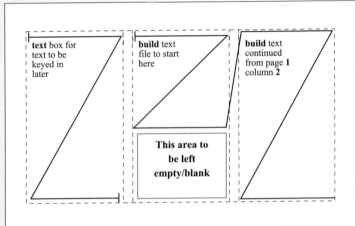

Page 2

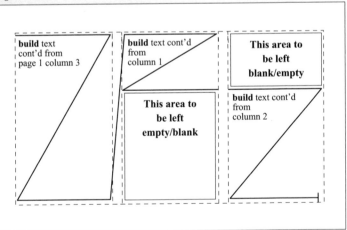

FIGURE 4.19 Page layout sketches

3 Import the text file **build** and position it as shown in the page layout sketch above.

Note that the text must start in column **2** of page **1**.

4 Save the publication using the filename **import**

5 Close the publication.

ASSESS YOUR SKILLS – Use design briefs, layout guides and text flow diagrams to display page content

By working through Section 2 you will have learnt how to:

- ○ work with design briefs and page layout guides
- ○ position ruler guides
- ○ remove ruler guides
- ○ import (insert) an image
- ○ resize an image while maintaining proportion
- ○ resize an image to an exact size
- ○ move images
- ○ layer images
- ○ work with text flow diagrams
- ○ insert text
- ○ turn off hyphenation
- ○ create text boxes
- ○ insert pages
- ○ delete pages
- ○ import (insert) a text file and control text flow.

If you think that you need more practice on any of the skills in the above list, go back and work through those skills again.

If you feel confident move on to Section 3.

Section 3: Create and use style sheets and correct text according to proof correction symbols

In this section you will learn how to:

- ○ understand style sheets
- ○ remove styles
- ○ create new styles
- ○ find text
- ○ apply styles to text
- ○ amend/change a style
- ○ amend text according to proof correction symbols.

Understanding text styles and style sheets

A text style is a set of formatting instructions that you can apply to text. You can apply a text style to an entire publication, or to a particular paragraph. A style sheet contains all text formatting information: font, font size, font emphasis, font colour, indents, alignment, character, line spacing, tabs and special formatting (e.g. numbered lists).

Creating a style sheet is the most efficient way of applying styles to text. Once you have created a style you can apply it to the text in one easy step.

A style sheet allows you to make changes to a text style throughout a publication by amending the style in the style sheet. When a style is changed, all the text in the publication displayed in that style will change to reflect the amendments made in the style sheet.

You will usually need to create three different styles for use in your publication: one for the body text, one for the subheadings and one for the heading.

You will be given specific instructions about the font family (serif or sans serif), size, emphasis, alignment and colour for each style but you can also set some options that will assist you in displaying your publication effectively.

Text prepared for desktop publishing is usually prepared with no clear line space between paragraphs. You should never use the Enter key to create this space – if required, paragraph spacing can be used to create space after paragraphs, subheadings and/or headings. You can experiment with

> **What does it mean?**
>
> **Style sheet**
> A style sheet is a collection of different styles to be used in the publication.

the spacing after paragraphs, however, some guidance on suitable options to set for each style is given below.

Body text

Spacing after paragraphs – Applying 2pt–6pt spacing after paragraphs will enable you to easily identify where a paragraph begins and ends.

First line indent – As an alternative to setting space after paragraphs, paragraphs can have a first line indent. When this option is set the first line of every paragraph will be inset from the left edge of the text box. Setting the first line indent to 0.5–1cm is usually sufficient.

Widows and orphans – There should never be a single line of a paragraph at the top of a page or column (widow) or a single line of a paragraph at the bottom of a page or column (orphan). To avoid widows and orphans set **widow/orphan control**.

Leading (pronounced ledding) – Leading is the technical term for the spacing between lines of text. Adjusting the space between lines of text can assist in ensuring that the text fills all available space in the publication. The space between lines can be set to three decimal places so that very fine adjustments can be made (e.g. 1.005pt). You will learn how adjust this in the next section.

Subheadings

Spacing after paragraphs – Applying 2pt–6pt spacing after paragraphs will create a space after each subheading.

Keep with next – Subheadings should never be positioned at the bottom of a page or column. Selecting the **Keep with next** option will prevent subheadings being positioned at the bottom of a page/column.

Heading

Spacing after paragraphs – Applying 2pt–6pt spacing after paragraphs will create a space under the heading.

Before you create a new style sheet you are advised to remove all existing styles so that you do not accidentally apply an existing style.

▶▶ How to... *remove styles*

1   Click on the **Format** menu.

2   Click on **Styles and Formatting**.

3   The **Styles and Formatting Task Pane** will be displayed on the left of the screen.

> **What does it mean?**
>
> **Leading**
> Leading is the technical term for the spacing between lines of text. In the old printing presses bars of lead were used to separate the lines of type.

4   In the **Styles and Formatting Task Pane** click on the drop-down arrow next to the **Show** box, then select **All Styles**.

5   Hover over the bottom style in the list, the style will be outlined in blue and a drop-down arrow will be displayed (Figure 4.20).

6   Click on the drop-down arrow next to the last style on the list, a drop-down menu will be displayed.

7   From the drop-down menu, click on **Delete**.

8   A dialogue box will appear asking if you want to delete the style, click on **Yes**.

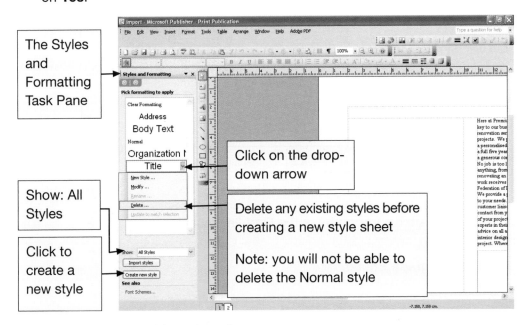

FIGURE 4.20 The styles and formatting task pane

9   Repeat steps 5 to 8 until all styles have been deleted (the Normal style cannot be deleted).

▶▶ How to... *create new styles*

1   Click on the **Format** menu.

2   Click on **Styles and Formatting**.

3   The **Styles and Formatting Task Pane** will be displayed on the left of the screen.

4   Ensure that all existing styles have been deleted (see above).

5   In the **Styles and Formatting Task Pane**, click on **Create new style** the **New Style** window will display.

6 In the box under **Enter new style name** type in the name of the style.

7 Click on the drop-down arrow next to the box under **Style for the following paragraph** and select **Normal**.

8 Click on **Font**. The **Font** dialogue box will be displayed (Figure 4.21).

9 Select the font, emphasis, size and colour for the style (the approximate appearance of the style will be shown in the **Sample** box).

10 Click on **OK**. You will be returned to the **New Style** window.

11 Click on **Paragraph,** the **Paragraph** dialogue box will be displayed (Figure 4.22).

12 In the box next to **Alignment** click on the drop-down arrow and select the alignment.

13 If required, set the spacing **After paragraphs** or the **First line** indent and space **Between lines**.

14 Click on the **Line and Paragraph Breaks** tab.

> Click on the drop-down arrow and select font

> Click on the drop-down arrow and select emphasis

> Click on the drop-down arrow and select size

> Click on drop-down arrow and select colour

> A sample of the style will be displayed

FIGURE 4.21 Formatting the font

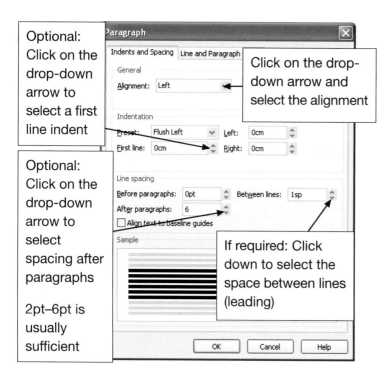

> Optional: Click on the drop-down arrow to select a first line indent

> Click on the drop-down arrow and select the alignment

> Optional: Click on the drop-down arrow to select spacing after paragraphs
>
> 2pt–6pt is usually sufficient

> If required: Click down to select the space between lines (leading)

FIGURE 4.22 Formatting body text

15 Click in the box to select the appropriate options for the style (Figure 4.23).

16 Click on **OK.**

17 You will be returned to the **New Style** window, click on **OK**.

18 Repeat from step 5 to step 17 until all styles have been created.

19 Click on **OK.**

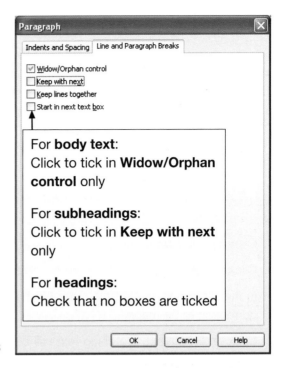

FIGURE 4.23 Line and paragraph options

1 Open the publication **import.**

2 Create the following text styles:

   Body text:
style:	**sans serif**
size:	**9pt**
emphasis:	**regular/normal**
colour:	**black**
alignment:	**left**

   Set the following options:
first line indent	**0.5 cm**
widow and orphan control	**on** (tick in the box)
Subheadings:	
style:	**serif**
size:	**12pt**
emphasis:	**bold only**
alignment:	**centre**
colour:	**blue**

   Set the following options:
space after paragraphs	**3pt**
keep with next **on** (tick in the box)	

3 Save the publication as **styles.**

4 Do not close the publication.

TIP!

Remember to delete all existing styles before creating the new styles.

Applying styles to text

Once the style sheet has been created the styles need to be applied to the text. The body text should be applied to all the text in the publication to avoid any paragraphs being missed. After the body text has been applied the other styles can be applied to the appropriate parts of the text.

You may find it helpful to use the find facility to locate the text to be set in a certain style.

▶▶ How to... *find text*

1 Click on the **Edit** menu.

2 Click on **Find.** The task pane will be displayed on the left of the screen.

3 In the task pane, in the box under **Find what** enter a phrase near the correction to be made.

4 Click on **Find Next.** Matching text will be highlighted in the publication.

5 Check that the correct phrase has been found (if not, click on **Find Next** until the correct phrase has been located).

6 Close the task pane.

TIP!

Read the text carefully to make sure that you have found the correct text.

▶▶ How to... *apply styles to text*

To apply the **body text**

1 Ensure the **Styles and Formatting Task Pane** is displayed.

2 Click anywhere in the text to be formatted.

3 Press **Ctrl+A** (all the text will be highlighted – it will be displayed with a black background).

TIP!

To display the Styles and Formatting Task Pane: click on **Format → ** click on **Styles and Formatting**.

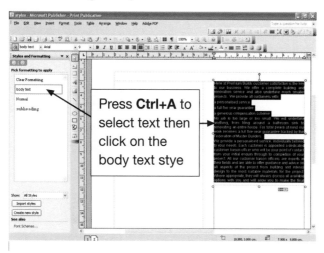

Press **Ctrl+A** to select text then click on the body text stye

FIGURE 4.24 Applying the body text style

4 In the **Styles and Formatting Task Pane** click on the body text style. The body text style will now be applied.

5   Click on the desktop area (the grey area around the publication).

To apply the subheading style

6   Click anywhere in the first subheading.

7   In the **Styles and Formatting Task Pane** click on the subheading style. The subheading style will now be applied.

8   Click in the next subheading and repeat step 7.

9   Repeat step 8 until the subheading style has been applied to all subheadings.

10 Click on the desktop area (the grey area around the publication).

To apply the heading style

11 Click anywhere in the heading.

12 In the **Styles and Formatting Task Pane** click on the heading style, the heading style will now be applied.

13 Click on the desktop area (the grey area around the publication).

14 After applying all styles, check the publication to ensure that all text is displayed in the publication.

> **TIP!**
>
> Clicking on the desktop deselects the style so that you do not accidentally apply it to a different part of the text.

> **TIP!**
>
> If you make a mistake, click on the **Undo** icon or click on the appropriate style in the style sheet and the previous style will be re-applied.

Check your understanding *Apply styles to text*

1   Continue working in the publication **styles**.

2   Apply the **body text** style to all the text in the publication.

3   Apply the subheading style to the following subheadings:

   - Consultation
   - Building Work
   - Painting and decorating
   - Carpentry
   - Plastering
   - Plumbing
   - Electrical Work
   - Special Services

> **TIP!**
>
> Check the final words in the text to ensure that all text is fully displayed.

4   Check that all the text is displayed in the publication – you may need to flow the text into the final text box.

5   Save the publication using the filename **apply**

6   Do not close the publication.

Making amendments to styles

Once styles have been applied, you may need to make adjustments, for example to increase or decrease the spacing after paragraphs or between lines to help fit the publication of the page, or to correct any errors you have made.

1   Ensure the **Styles and Formatting Task Pane** is displayed.

2   In the **Styles and Formatting Task Pane** hover over the style to be changed, click on the drop-down arrow at the end of the box containing the style name to display a drop-down menu.

3   Select **Modify** from the drop-down menu.

4   The **Modify Style** dialogue box will display.

5   Click on **Font** and/or **Paragraph** and make the necessary changes.

6   Click on **OK** to return to the **Modify Style** dialogue box. Click **OK**. All text displayed in that style will be updated automatically.

7   Check the publication carefully to ensure that all text is displayed in the publication.

Check your understanding *Modify text styles*

1   Continue working in the publication **styles**.

2   Make the following changes to the **body text** style:

   ○ alignment: **justified**
   ○ first line indent: **0 cm**
   ○ space after paragraphs: **3pt**

3   Make the following changes to the **subheading** style:

   ○ emphasis: **bold and italic**
   ○ alignment: **left**

4   Save the publication using the filename **modify**

5   Close the publication.

Amending text according to proof correction symbols

You will need to make corrections to text. You need to familiarise yourself with the following proof correction symbols:

New paragraph ⌐ or // or ⌐
Click immediately in front of the word that is to start the new paragraph, then press the Enter key **once**. Check that there is no space at the start of the new paragraph.

Run on ⌐‿‿‿‿)
Click immediately in front of the word that begins the new paragraph then press the Backspace key. Check that there is one space after the punctuation that ended the first paragraph.

What does it mean?

Run on
Run on means removing the paragraph break so that two paragraphs become one.

Insertion ⋏ with a second ⋏ and words to be inserted in margin
Click immediately in front of the word where the text is to be added.
Enter the required text. Check that the spacing between words and after
punctuation is correct.

Insert space ⋏ with # ⋏ or ⊤ in margin
Click in the position that the space is to be inserted, then press the
Spacebar once.

Transpose horizontally ⌐⌐
Highlight the first word(s) and the following space identified by the symbol
(e.g. it is), position the mouse over the selected word(s), click and drag
the word(s) to the new location. Check spacing before and after the
amendment.

Transpose vertically ⌐ or ∞
Highlight the text identified by the bottom oval or line, position the mouse
over the selected text, click and drag the selected text to the new location.
Alternatively, select the text identified by the top oval or line, position the
mouse over the selected text, click and drag the selected text to the new
location. Check spacing before and after the amendment.

Close up ⌒
Click immediately in front of the space to be deleted then press the Delete
key *or* click immediately after the space to be deleted then press the
Backspace key.

Stet — — — — with ⊘ in margin

The words underlined with a broken line should be kept in the publication.
Normally, nothing will need to be corrected.

Delete —— through character(s) with ⌒⌐ in margin
Highlight the text that has been crossed out with a line, press the Delete *or*
the Backspace key.

Set in capitals ≡ under character(s)
Highlight the letter(s) to be set in capitals then click on the **Format** menu
→ **Font** in the **Effects** section, click to place a tick in the box to the left of
All caps → **OK**.

(lines of text
that are to be bulleted   } Apply bullets to these lines of text
enclosed in brackets)

with instruction next to bracket

▶▶ How to... *insert bullets*

1   Locate the text to be bulleted (you may find it helpful to use the find
facility, see page 32).

What does it mean?

Transpose
Transpose means
changing the text around
so that the identified
word(s)/lines swap
places.

What does it mean?

Close up
Close up means to
remove the space.

What does it mean?

Stet
Stet means to leave the
text as it was before the
correction was made.

TIP!

Before applying bullets
check that the font
style and size are as
specified. If you need
to re-apply the previous
style after applying
bullets, you will also
need to re-apply the
bullets.

2   Select or highlight the lines to be bulleted.

3   On the **Formatting toolbar**, click on the **bullets** icon ⠿.

4   Check that the spacing above and below the bulleted text is correct.

5   Click on the **Save** icon.

▶▶ *How to...* *amend the spacing between bullets and the*
text (optional)

1   Select bulleted text (ensure all lines of the bulleted text are
    highlighted).

2   On the **Ruler**, click and hold on the **Indent Marker**.

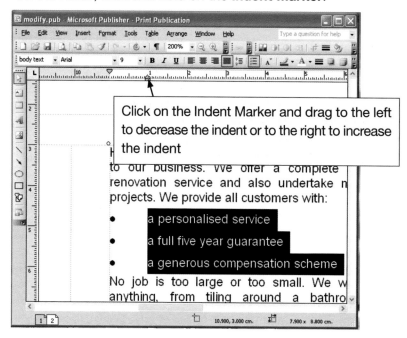

FIGURE 4.25 Adjusting the spacing between the bullets and the text

3   Drag the Indent Marker to the required position. The text will move to
    this new position.

4   Click away from the bullet text to deselect the bulleted text.

▶▶ *How to...* *amend text*

1   Locate the text that is to be amended (you may find it helpful to use
    the find facility, see How to... find text on page 32).

2   Make the required amendment.

3   Check the spacing before and after the amendment.

4   Click on the **Save** icon.

TIP!

After making
amendments, check
that the spacing
before and after the
amendment is correct.
There should be only
one space after a full
stop, question mark or
exclamation mark.

1 Open the publication **modify**.

2 Make the corrections shown below:

Here at Premium Builds customer satisfaction is the key to our business. We offer a complete building and renovation service and also undertake much smaller projects. We provide all customers with:

a personalised service

a full five year guarantee

a generous compensation scheme

> Apply bullets to these 3 lines of text

No job is too large or too small. We will undertake anything, from tiling around a bathroom sink to renovating an entire house. For total peace of mind our work receives a full five-year guarantee backed by the Federation of Master Builders.

We provide a personalised service, individually tailored to your needs. Each customer is assigned a dedicated customer liaison officer who will be the point of contact from the initial enquiry through to completion of the project. All our customer liaison officers are experts in their fields and are able to offer guidance and advice on all aspects of the project from building and interior design to the most suitable materials for the project. Where appropriate, they will always discuss all available options with you and will allow you to make the final decisions about the work to be completed. You will be given a realistic timescale for the project and if these timescales are not adhered to, we offer a generous compensation scheme.

For complete peace of mind, we only ask you to pay a small deposit to cover the cost of materials at the start of the contract. The balance is payable only when the work is completed to your entire satisfaction.

of charge

Consultation

All initial consultations are free During the initial consultation, you will have an opportunity to browse though our extensive portfolio of work completed and to view letters of recommendation from satisfied clients. This consultation will enable you to meet the customer liaison officer who will take responsibility for your project. The liaison officer will listen to your needs and, if required, draw up plans and discuss all the options available to you. We have access to discount suppliers of materials and can help you to keep the costs down by passing this trade discount on to you without sacrificing quality. Of course, if you prefer, you may provide the materials yourself.

Building Work

Having building work carried out on your home can be a very stressful, complicated process from beginning to end. We aim to minimise the disruption to your day-to-day life. Our consultants will keep you informed every step of the way and if additional work is required this will be explained in full. At the end of each working day our builders will clear the working area and will ensure that tools and dangerous objects are stored out of the reach of children. Safety is always our top priority.

Painting and decorating

We pride ourselves in providing a very professional service. All surfaces will be thoroughly cleaned and/or stripped down and any areas in need of attention will be made good, ensuring a professional finish. Most work can be started within two weeks of your initial enquiry and we will give you a realistic estimate of the time it will take to complete the job.

Carpentry

Our highly skilled carpenters can provide for all your carpentry needs. We can design and make fitted furniture for any room at very competitive prices, using materials to suit your design and budget. We also specialise in designing and installing laminate and hardwood floors. We take pride in finding a solution for even the most challenging surfaces.

Plastering

We offer a plastering service for both internal and external walls and surfaces. Whether you require a full re-plaster, a simple repair to existing plastering, restoration of damaged cornices, or an ornate plasterwork design, our plasterers are experts in their field and will be happy to discuss your needs and offer innovative solutions.

Plumbing

A good plumber can be hard to find. You need look no further. With all work guaranteed for at least five years you can have confidence in the service that we provide. Our plumbers can install complete heating and water systems or solve everyday plumbing problems – from a blocked sink to the relocation of appliances.

Electrical Work

Safety is our first concern. Whether you need extra plug sockets or a complete rewire, our electricians are here to help. We have electricians who are experienced in installing special effect lighting, for example ascending ankle-height staircase lights set on sensors, mood lighting for bathrooms and living areas, or outside lighting for gardens and patios. All work is carried out to the highest standards and surfaces will be made good after the work has been completed. You will receive an NIC electrical safety certificate after completion of any electrical project.

Special Services

During the completion of any work we will endeavour to keep disruption to your life minimal. If you are in full-time work, you may either leave your keys with us so that our employees can enter your premises at the start of each working day or, if you prefer, our contractors will arrive before you leave each morning so that you can let them in. At the end of each working day our contractors will, as far as possible, clear and clean the working area and will ensure that your premises are secure before leaving. Our contractors do not normally work on Saturday or Sunday, however, if you have an urgent project, or if you wish the project to be quickly completed, we can arrange for work to continue over the weekend. There may be an extra charge for this service. Where our contractors are undertaking major building work, they will erect temporary structures to ensure your premises are water-tight and secure at all times. They will ensure that you have the basic amenities to continue to live in your premises. You may however prefer to vacate the premises whilst the most disruptive work is carried out. We have made arrangements with a major hotel chain to accommodate clients in their hotels at a considerably discounted rate.

Should you wish to avail yourself of this facility, your customer liaison officer will be pleased to discuss the details and make the arrangements for you.

3 Save the publication using the filename **correct**

4 Close the publication.

ASSESS YOUR SKILLS – Create and use style sheets and correct text according to proof correction symbols

By working through Section 3 you will have learnt how to:

- ○ understand style sheets
- ○ remove styles
- ○ create new styles
- ○ find text
- ○ apply styles to text
- ○ amend/change a style
- ○ amend text according to proof correction symbols.

If you think that you need more practice on any of the skills in the above list, go back and work through those skills again.

If you feel confident move on to Section 4.

Section 4: Create special text effects, fomat objects and produce a variety of publications

LEARNING OUTCOMES

In this section you will learn how to:

- ○ apply a dropped/raised capital
- ○ rotate text
- ○ reverse text
- ○ create WordArt
- ○ insert and format lines and arrows
- ○ insert and format boxes
- ○ group and ungroup objects
- ○ copy, paste and move grouped objects.

Creating special text effects

Special text effects can enhance your publication. You may be asked to apply a specific text effect or you may be given the option of applying a special effect of your choice. Examples of special effects are:

Dropped or raised capitals

The first letter of a paragraph is either raised or dropped below the line on which it is situated to give emphasis to the paragraph. A dropped capital drops at least one line below the line on which it is situated, whereas a raised capital is raised at least one line above the line on which it is situated.

Reverse text

Text is shown in white on a contrasting (often black) background. Do not confuse reverse text with rotated text or text keyed in backwards.

Word Art

Publisher has a set of predefined effects that can be applied to text, they include shaped text, 3-D effects, embossing and shadows.

▶▶ How to... *apply a dropped or raised capital*

1 Click anywhere in the paragraph to which you want to apply a dropped or raised capital.

2 Click on the **Format** menu.

3 Click on **Drop Cap**.

4 The Drop Cap dialogue box will display (Figure 4.26).

5 Select a style.

6 If required, click on the **Custom Drop Cap** tab.

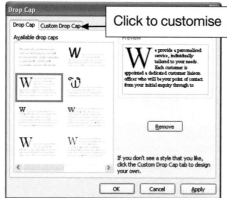
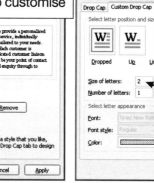

FIGURE 4.26 Applying dropped capitals

7 In the box next to **Size of letters** enter the number of lines high you wish the dropped/raised capital to be.

8 Click on **Apply**.

9 Click on **OK**.

▶▶ How to... *rotate text*

1 Click on the text box containing the text to be rotated.

2 The handles of the text box will be displayed.

TIP!

For short paragraphs select a two-line dropped capital.

3 On the **Standard Toolbar** click on the drop-down arrow to the right of the **Free Rotate** icon ⟲ ▾ .

4 Select the required rotation (usually **Rotate Left 90°**).

5 Adjust the text box to fit the area for the rotated text.

▶▶ How to... *reverse text*

1 Select (highlight) the text to be reversed.

2 On the **Formatting Toolbar** click on the drop-down arrow to the right of the **Font Color** icon **A** ▾ .

3 From the drop-down menu click on the white square (the text will not be visible).

4 On the **Formatting Toolbar** click on the drop-down arrow to the right of the **Fill Color** icon ⬧ ▾ .

5 From the drop-down menu click on the required background colour (usually black).

6 The text will be displayed in white on a contrasting background.

Check your understanding *Apply dropped capitals*

1 Open the publication **correct**.

2 Apply a two-line dropped capital to the first and last paragraphs of text.

3 Save the publication using the filename **special**

4 Do not close the publication.

Check your understanding *Use reverse text*

1 Continue working in the publication **special**.

2 In the text box in column 1 of page 1 key in the text:

PREMIUM BUILDS

(you may use any font style for this text, the text may be displayed on two lines).

3 Rotate this text 90° to the left.

4 Use the text box handles to adjust the text box so that it fills column 1, as it did before the text was rotated.

5 Re-size the text so that it is fills most of the height of the column.

6 Reverse this text.

7 Save the publication keeping the filename **special**.

8 Close the publication.

TIP!

To fit text to a single unconnected text box, select the text box, click on **Format menu** → AutoFit Text → Best Fit.

1   On the **Objects toolbar** click on the **Insert WordArt** icon ![icon].

2   The WordArt Gallery will be displayed.

3   Click on the required style then click on **OK**.

4   The **Edit WordArt Text** dialogue box will display (Figure 4.27).

5   Key in the required text.

6   Select the font, size and emphasis, if required.

7   Click on **OK**.

8   The text will be converted to an image and can be moved and resized in the same way (refer to page 15).

9   Move the text to the required position and resize if necessary.

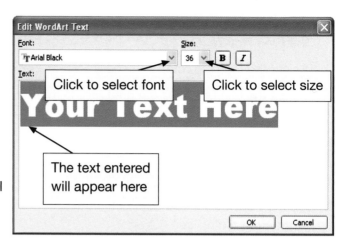

FIGURE 4.27 Creating WordArt

Inserting and formatting lines, arrows and boxes

You can draw lines, boxes and arrows anywhere in your publication. These can then be formatted to suit your requirements. Unless instructed otherwise, you must check that these objects do not touch or overlap any other page items.

1   On the **Objects toolbar** click on the **Line** \ or the **Arrow** icon 🢅.

2   The mouse pointer changes to a cross +.

3   Move the mouse to the position where the line/arrow should begin.

4   Click and drag to draw a line/arrow of the required size.

5   To draw a straight line/arrow, hold down the **Shift** key whilst drawing the line.

6   When the line is the required size, release the mouse button then release the **Shift** key.

7   Ensure the line/arrow is selected (handles will appear at either end).

8   Position the mouse over the line/arrow then right-click.

9   From the drop-down menu that displays select **Format Autoshape**. The Format **AutoShape** dialogue box will display (Figure 4.28).

TIP!

The same method is used to apply text wrap to images and other page objects.

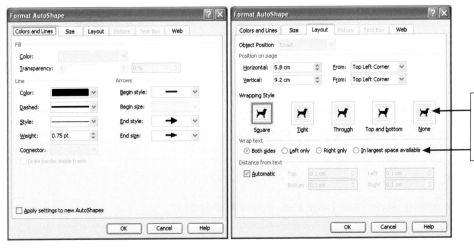

FIGURE 4.28 Formatting lines and arrows, and wrapping text

Select how you wish text to wrap around the arrow/line

10 In turn, click on the drop-down arrows next to **Color**, **Dashed**, **Style** and **Weight** to select the required settings for the line.

11 For arrows click on **Begin Style** and/or **End Style** to select the required settings for the arrow.

12 Click on the **Layout Tab**.

13 Select the required **Wrapping Style**.

14 If necessary, select the **Wrap Text** required (where you want text to be displayed around the arrow/line).

▶▶ How to... *insert and format boxes*

1 On the **Objects toolbar,** click on the **Rectangle**.

2 The mouse pointer changes to a cross +.

3 Move the mouse to the position where the top-left corner of the box is to be placed.

4 Click and drag to draw the box to the required size.

5 To draw a square box, hold down the **Shift** key whilst drawing.

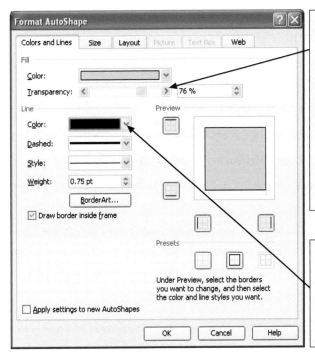

To shade a box click down to select the **color** (black, red, green or blue) then hold and slide the bar to adjust the **Transparency**. Do NOT choose a colour that is not used in the publication

To create a box without lines click on the drop-down arrow next to **color** and select **No Line**

FIGURE 4.29 Formatting a box

6   When the box is the required size, release the mouse button.

7   Ensure the box is selected (handles will appear around the box).

8   Position the mouse over the box then right-click.

9   From the drop-down menu that displays, click on **Format** AutoShape. The **Format AutoShape** dialogue box will display.

10 Click on the **Colors and Lines** tab to select the **Fill** and **Line** colour and design.

11 Click on the **Layout Tab**.

12 Select the required **Wrapping Style** (see How to… insert and format lines and arrows on page 42).

13 If necessary, select the **Wrap Text** required (where you want text to be displayed around the box).

14 If required, layer the box (select the box ➜ right-click ➜ **Order** ➜ select required order).

Check your understanding *Insert and format lines, arrows and boxes*

1   Open the publication **images**.

2   You will continue working on the Master Page.

3   Display the Master Page.

4   Use WordArt to display the text **Premium Builds** at the top centre of the publication between the toolbox and the paint pot images.

5   Make sure that the words do not touch or overlap any of the images, the top page margin or bottom ruler guide.

6   Draw a box around all the page items. The box should touch but not overlap the top, left and bottom margin guides and the bottom ruler guide.

7   Format the box to have a light shading (75–90%), with no lines.

8   Ensure that the box is displayed behind all other page items (**Order** ➜ **Send to back**).

9   Draw a vertical, downward-pointing arrow approximately 1 cm long.

10 Position this arrow so it is under the words Premium Builds and touches the bottom of the shaded box.

11 Format the arrow to have a 3pt solid line, you may select any arrow head **End style** and **End size** (the **Begin style** must be a straight line).

12 Save the publication using the filename **art**

13 Do not close the publication.

1 On the **Objects toolbar,** click on the **Select objects** icon ▨.

2 With the pointer draw a box that fully encloses all the items to be grouped (note: any objects that are not fully enclosed within the box will not be selected).

3 When you release the mouse the objects will be selected and the **Group Objects** icon will be displayed below the selected items.

4 Click on the **Group Objects** icon 🔲 the objects will be grouped.

5 To ungroup the items click on the **Ungroup Objects** icon 🔲 the objects will be ungrouped and the icon will change to the **Group Objects** icon 🔲.

6 To regroup click on the **Group Objects** icon again.

You can also select each item to be grouped by holding down the Shift key then clicking on each item to be grouped. When all items are selected, release the Shift key.

TIP!

Take care not to move any of the items once they have been ungrouped

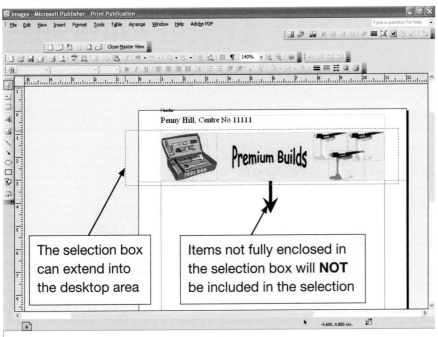

FIGURE 4.30 Selecting objects

The selection box can extend into the desktop area

Items not fully enclosed in the selection box will **NOT** be included in the selection

1 Select the grouped items by clicking anywhere on top of the grouped items, handles will appear around the grouped objects.

2 Click on the **Copy** 🗐 icon.

3 Click on the **Paste** 🗐 icon.

4 A copy of the grouped objects will appear in the publication.

5 Position the mouse on top of the *copy* of the grouped items the cursor will change to ✛ .

6 Click and drag the grouped objects to move them to the required position.

7 Click on the desktop to deselect the copied items.

1 Continue working in the publication **art**.

2 You will continue working on the Master Page.

3 Group the shaded box, all the images and the text Premium Builds (the header and the arrow should not be included in the group).

4 Copy the grouped items.

5 Move the *copy* of the grouped items to the bottom of the publication.

6 The grouped items should touch, but not overlap, the bottom, left and right margins.

7 Save the publication using the filename **group**

8 Close the publication.

ASSESS YOUR SKILLS – Create special text effects, format objects and produce a variety of publications

By working through Section 4 you will have learnt how to:

- apply a dropped/raised capital
- rotate text
- reverse text
- create WordArt
- insert and format lines and arrows
- insert and format boxes
- group and ungroup objects
- copy, paste and move grouped objects.

If you think that you need more practice on any of the skills in the above list, go back and work through those skills again.

If you feel confident move on to Section 5.

LEARNING OUTCOMES

In this section you will learn how to:

○ copyfit a publication

○ adjust the leading (line spacing)

○ check the design of a publication

○ save a template

○ make a copy of a template

○ use a template to create a variety of publications

○ set up a publication to print colour separations

○ set crop marks to print

○ print a template

○ print a composite copy

○ print colour separations.

Copyfitting a publication

Copyfitting the publication means fitting the page content to the exact amount of space allocated for the publication, without breaking any of the 'design rules' specified by the publisher.

There are many techniques you can use to help copyfit the publication. The spacing between paragraphs and/or between lines (leading) can be increased or decreased. Images may also be re-sized, but you must ensure that the original proportions are maintained and that the image is still large enough for it to be clearly seen.

The 'design rules' may vary from publisher to publisher and from one publication to another (for example, in some circumstances 'white space' is used to create a visual impact, and in some circumstances it will be acceptable to have hyphenated line endings). However, in most circumstances you will need to ensure that your publication is copyfitted to ensure that:

What does it mean?

White space
'White space' is the space on a page that is not covered by print or graphic matter (the space is not necessarily white).

○ there is no more than 10 mm of vertical white space anywhere in the publication

○ leading (line spacing) is consistent*

○ paragraph spacing is consistent*

○ there are no hyphenated line endings*

○ subheadings are kept with related text*

○ there are no widows or orphans*

- all material is displayed as specified
- the text file is displayed in full
- proportions of images have been maintained.

The objects marked with * should have been included in the style sheet and will be applied automatically when the styles are applied to the text (see 'Understanding text styles and style sheets' on page XX). However, you may still need to adjust the leading (space between lines) to ensure that the publication fills all the available space.

Publisher has a design checker that will allow you to check for the most obvious problems in your publication, for example, text not displayed in full or out-of-proportion graphics. In some cases you will be offered an option to automatically fix the problem but for others you will need to fix the problem yourself. You will still need to check the publication yourself, but this will assist you in fixing the most obvious problems.

▶▶ How to... adjust the leading (line-spacing)

1 Ensure the final text box of the publication is displayed on the screen (this will help you see how much space you need to fill or create).

2 Ensure the **Styles and Formatting Task Pane** is displayed.

3 In the **Styles and Formatting Task Pane** hover over the style to be changed (usually body text), a blue box with a drop-down arrow at the end will be displayed.

4 Click on the arrow, a drop-down list will appear.

5 Click on **Modify.**

6 The **Modify Style** dialogue box will be displayed.

7 In the Click to Change section, click on **Paragraph.**

8 Click in the box at the end of **Between lines** and enter the required measurement.

9 Click on **OK**, then click on **OK** again.

10 Check your publication to see whether the adjustment is sufficient to fill the publication.

11 Click on the final text box in the publication. If [A ···] is shown at the bottom of the text box some text may not be displayed, and you will need to decrease the leading until all text is visible.

12 If required repeat steps 3 to 11 until the text fills the publication.

TIP!

Remember that the line spacing can be adjusted to 3 decimal places (e.g. 1.015 mm).

TIP!

Try a small adjustment first (e.g. 1.11 mm to increase or 0.99 mm to decrease) to see the effect.

1   Click on the **Tools** menu.

2   Click on **Design Checker**. The **Design Checker Task Pane** is displayed.

3   Look at the problems identified (if any).

> Any problems will be listed in the Design Checker Task Pane

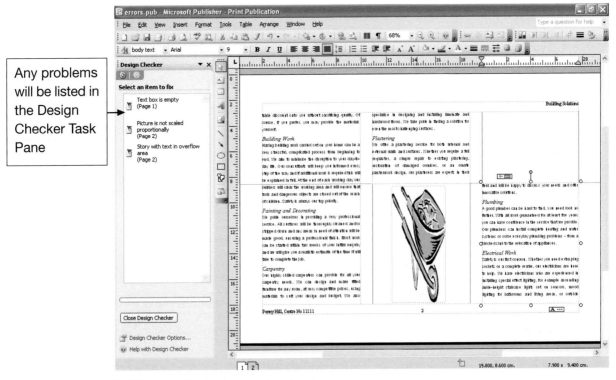

FIGURE 4.31 The Design Checker Task Pane

4   Hover the mouse over the listed problem and click on the drop-down arrow that appears at the end of the box.

For 'Text box is empty'

- Click on **Go to this Item**

- Check whether the text box should be empty – if so ignore the problem

- if not, press the Delete key to delete the text box.

For 'Picture is not scaled proportionally'

- Click on **Fix: Rescale Picture**

For 'Story with text in overflow area'

- Click on **Go to this Item**

- Check whether the text box needs to be enlarged or whether you need to adjust the leading (line spacing) of the body text style. Make the necessary adjustment(s).

> **TIP!**
>
> Images may also be resized to assist in the copyfitting process.

5   Repeat step 4 until all problems have been fixed.

6   Repeat steps 1 to 3 to check that all problems have been fixed (if any problems remain repeat steps 3 to 6 again).

Check your understanding *Copyfitting a publication*

1   Open the publication **special**.

2   Adjust the leading of the body text to ensure that there is no more than 10 mm of vertical white space anywhere in the publication (except where specified: the bottom of column 2 on page 1, the bottom of column 2 and the top of column 3 on page 2).

3   Check that column 1 and column 3 on page 2 are balanced to within 10 mm (1 cm).

4   Run the design checker to ensure that there are no obvious problems in your publication.

5   Check your publication to ensure that:

   ○ leading is consistent
   ○ paragraph spacing is consistent
   ○ there are no widows or orphans
   ○ subheadings are not displayed at the bottom of any column
   ○ there are no hyphenated line endings
   ○ all the text is displayed in full.

6   Correct any problems by:

   ○ checking that all styles have been applied to the appropriate parts of the text
   ○ checking the style sheet has been set up correctly
   ○ checking that hyphenation has been turned off.

7   Save your publication using the filename **copyfit**

8   Close the publication.

Check your understanding *Checking the proportion of images*

1   Open your saved publication **group.**

2   Use the Design Checker to ensure that all images are in proportion.

   Note: Publisher may find three possible problems:
   ○ the footer is empty
   ○ the box at the top of the publication is shaded (object has transparency)
   ○ the box at the bottom of the publication is shaded.

   These are all intentional and should be ignored!

3   If any additional problems are found, make the necessary correction(s).

4   Save the publication keeping the filename **group**.

5   Close the publication.

Saving a template

In Publisher, it is possible to save a publication as a template. One advantage of saving a publication as a template is that it is only possible to open a *copy* of a template, preventing the original publication from being altered by accident. However, template files are automatically saved in a templates folder that is not always accessible to users; therefore in this book we will save template documents as publications and will create the template by making the file a 'read only' file to avoid accidental amendments to the original file.

▶▶ How to... *save a template*

1 Save the publication in the normal way (see Section 1, page 8).

2 Close the publication.

3 From **My Computer**, locate the file that is to be used as a template.

4 Click on the file.

5 Click on the **File** menu.

6 Click on **Properties**.

7 Click on the **General** tab.

8 In the box next to **Attributes**, click to put a tick in the box to the left of **Read-only**.

9 When the file is opened you will not be able to save the file with the same name unless the file is saved in a different location so the original file will be preserved.

Check your understanding *Save a template*

1 From **My Computer**, in your working area, locate your saved file **group**.

2 Set the attributes of this file to be **Read-only**.

▶▶ How to... *make a copy of a template*

1 Save the publication in the normal way (see Section 1 page 8).

2 Close the publication.

3 From **My Comput**er, locate the file that is to be copied.

4 Click on the file.

5 Click on the **Edit** menu.

6 Click on **Copy**.

7 Click on the **Edit** menu.

8 Click on **Paste**.

9 A *copy* of the file will be pasted in your working area, open the *copy* of the file when creating new publications.

1 From **My Computer,** in your working area, locate the file **group**.

2 Make a copy of this file.

▶▶ How to... *use a template to create a variety of publications*

1 Open a copy of the template (either the read-only file or the copy of the original file).

2 Check that page 1 of the publication is displayed on the screen (*not* the Master Page).

3 Insert the content of the publication.

4 Design check the publication (see 'How to... check the design of a publication', page 49).

5 Click on the **File** menu, then click on **Save As**.

6 Save the publication in the normal way (see 'How to... save a publication', page 8).

1 Open a copy of the template **group** (this may be the read-only **group** file or the **Copy of group** file).

2 Make sure page 1 is displayed on the screen.

3 Import the text file **work** in the white space in the centre of the publication (remember, you will need to draw a text box before you can insert the file).

4 **Centre** this text horizontally.

5 Display the text using fonts, styles and sizes to suit your publication.

6 Make sure that **all** the text is fully displayed and does not touch or overlap any page items.

7 Save the publication using the filename **jobs**

8 Open a copy of the template **group** (this may be the read-only **group** file or the **copy of group** file).

9 Make sure page 1 is displayed on the screen.

10 Import the text file **tenperct** in the white space in the centre of the publication.

11 Display the text using fonts, styles and sizes to suit your publication.

12 Make sure that **all** the text is fully displayed and does not touch or overlap any page items.

13 Save the publication using the filename **offers**

Preparing publications for press and printing templates, composite and colour-separated copies

Crop marks

Crop marks are guide marks that define the page edges and show the finishers where to trim the publication on the guillotine. Crop marks will only print on paper that is larger than the publication size. You will only be required to print crop marks on a small non-standard page size so the crop marks will show when printed on A4 paper.

Composite prints

A composite print is a print on which all the page items are displayed as they appear in the publication. The print need not be in colour, but if a black-and-white printer is used, all the page items must be displayed in full (any colours in the publication will be printed in shades of grey).

Colour separations

Colour separated prints allow professional printing companies to prepare different colour plates for use during the printing process (the inks are applied to the paper one ink at a time until all the colours combine to give a high quality finished product). Each colour used in a publication will appear on a separate page (for example, in a red and black publication the red items will be printed on one page and the black items on another page). Colour separated printouts are normally printed in black and white and the colour information is then printed (or written) on the print to indicate to the printer which colour ink is to be used in the printing process.

Colour separations can be prepared either as processed colours, Cyan, Magenta, Yellow and Black (CMYK) or as spot colours, Red, Green and Blue (RGB). Using CMYK is expensive but it enables all colours to be reproduced on the page. This process is generally used when a publication includes full colour photographs and/or detailed multi-coloured graphics. Using spot colours is a less expensive option and is frequently used in publications to emphasise headings, borders, logos and to produce line drawings or other simple graphics with a limited colour range.

You will be only be required to produce red, green and blue colour separations (spot colours) so all colours used in the publication will be converted to a shade of the colour(s) to be used in the printing process.

To print colour separations you may need to install a postscript printer driver called **Generic Color PS for Commercial Printing**.

Generic Color PS for Commercial Printing is not automatically installed on your system when you install Publisher. You must install it manually. You are advised to install this printer driver before you print colour-separated copies.

> **What does it mean?**
>
> **CMYK**
> CMYK stands for Cyan, Magenta, Yellow and Key. The Key colour (represented by the K) is black, as black is usually an essential ink in processed colour printing.

1 On the **Start** menu, click on **Printers and Faxes**.

2 Under **Printer Tasks**, click **Add a Printer**.

3 Follow the instructions in the **Add Printer Wizard**.

4 Under **Local or Network Printer**, select **Local printer attached to this computer**, and then make sure that the **Automatically detect and install my Plug and Play printer** check box is cleared.

5 Under **Install Printer Software**, click **Have Disk**.

6 In the **Install From Disk** dialogue box, click **Browse**, and then navigate to \Program Files\Microsoft Office\OFFICE11 on the drive where you have installed Publisher.

7 Select the file MSCOL11.INF, click **Open**, and then click **OK**.

Windows XP will install the printer driver **Generic Color PS for Commercial Printing** in your **Printers and Faxes** folder.

▶▶ How to... *set up a publication to print colour separations*

1 Open the publication to be printed.

2 Click on **Tools** menu.

3 Click on **Commercial Printing Tools**

4 Click on **Color Printing** the Color Printing dialogue box will display.

5 Click on **Spot Colors**, a dialogue box will be displayed (Figure 4.32).

6 Click on **OK**, you will be returned to the Color Printing dialogue box.

7 Check that the inks shown under the **Inks** tab are the correct colours to be used in the publication (if not you will need to cancel, amend the publication and repeat from step 2).

FIGURE 4.32 The Spot Colors dialogue box

8 Click on **OK**.

TIP!

When printing a colour-separated publication that is smaller than A4 it is advisable to print the **Job Information** as this displays the page number and whether the page is a black or spot colour page. **File → Print → Advanced Print Settings → Page Settings tab →** click on **Job Information** to place a tick in box.

1 Open the publication **copyfit**.

2 Prepare colour-separated printouts.

3 Save the publication using the filename **colsep**

▶▶ How to... *set crop marks to print*

1 Open the publication to be printed.

2 Click on the **File** menu.

3 Click on **Print**.

4 The Print dialogue box will be displayed.

5 Click on the **Advanced Print Settings** button.

6 Click on the **Page Settings** tab.

7 In the **Printer's Marks** section, click on **Crop marks** to place a tick in the box.

8 Click on **OK**.

9 The Print dialogue box will be displayed.

10 Follow the appropriate instructions for the type of print to be made.

▶▶ How to... *print a template or publication*

1 Open the template or publication to be printed.

2 If you are printing colour separations make sure that you have set up the publication for colour separations (How to... set up a publication to print colour separations, see page 54).

3 Click on the **File** menu.

4 Click on **Print**.

5 The Print dialogue box will be displayed.

6 *If* the **Change Copies Per Sheet** button is displayed, click **Change Copies Per Sheet**.

> If the **Change Copies Per Sheet...** button is displayed, click on the button to set the publication to be printed one per page

7 Click on **Print one copy per sheet**.

8 Click on **OK** you will be returned to the Print dialogue box.

9 Follow the appropriate instructions for the required printout.

TIP!

You can print the Master Page from page 1 or the Master Page (only the Master Page items will be present in the publication).

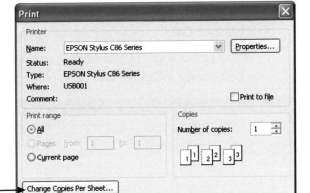

FIGURE 4.33 Changing the number of copies per sheet

To print a template
- In the print dialogue box, click on the **Print Range** section, select **Current Page**.
- Click on **OK**.

To print a composite copy
- In the print dialogue box click on the **Advanced Print Settings** button.
- Click on the **Separations** tab.
- Check that the **Output** is set to **Composite RGB** or **Composite Greyscale** (if not click on the drop-down arrow at the end of the box to select) then click on **OK**.
- The Print dialogue box will be displayed.
- In the **Print Range** section, click on **All**.
- Click on **OK**.

To print colour separations
- Click on the **Advanced Print Settings** button in the Print dialogue box.
- Click on the **Separations** tab.
- Click in the drop-down arrow at the end of the **Output** box and click on **Separations**.
- Click on the down arrow at the end of the **These plates** box and click on **Used Inks Only**.
- In the Print plate section, check that there is a tick in the box next to each colour to be printed (if not, click to add a tick).
- Click on **OK**.
- The Print dialogue box will be displayed.
- In the **Print Range** section, click on **All**.
- Click on **OK**.
- Your publication should print. If the dialogue box shown in Figure 4.34 is displayed you

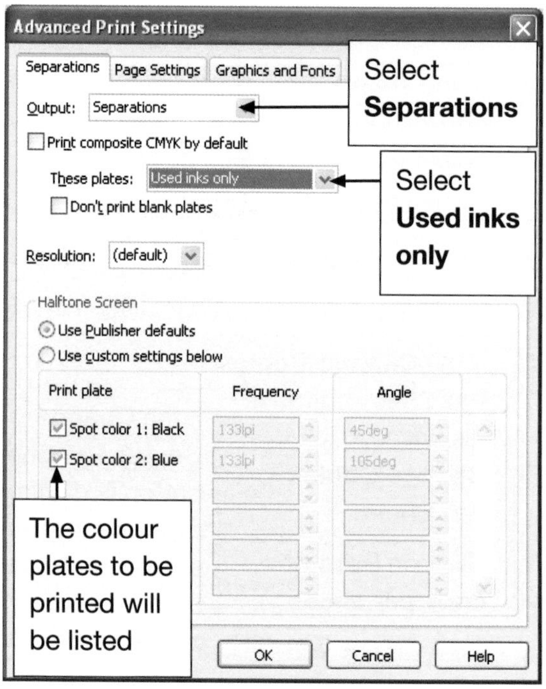

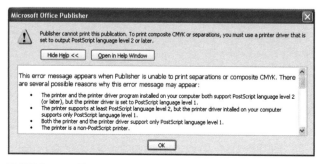

FIGURE 4.35 The print error screen

FIGURE 4.34 Printing colour separations

may submit a screen print from the Advanced Print Settings, Separations tab, showing the correct settings for your publication (it should look similar to the one shown in Figure 4.34) together with a composite print of the publication.

TIP!

The print settings will not always be retained when you close the document. If you open the document again you will need to check the print settings before printing.

Check your understanding *Print colour separations*

1 Open your saved publication **colsep**.

2 Print a colour-separated copy of the publication.

3 Check that one print shows **only** the blue items.

4 The colour of this printout must be shown on the print. You may need to handwrite the word '**blue**' on this printout.

5 Check that one print shows **only** the black items.

6 The colour of this printout must be shown on the print. You may need to handwrite the word '**black**' on this printout.

7 Save the publication using the filename **colsep**

TIP!

If any incorrect colours are listed in the print plate section, click **Cancel** and check that you have set up your publication for printing colour separations.

Check your understanding *Print a template*

1 Open your saved template **group**.

2 Print a copy of the template (there should be no page items on page 1).

3 Close the publication without saving.

Check your understanding *Print a publication*

1 Open your saved publication **offers**.

2 Print a **composite** copy of the publication.

3 Close the publication without saving.

Check your understanding *Set crop marks to print*

1 Open your saved publication **jobs**.

2 Set crop marks to print.

3 Print a **composite** copy of the publication showing crop marks.

4 Save the file keeping the filename **jobs**.

By working through Section 5 you will have learnt how to:

- ○ copyfit a publication
- ○ adjust the leading (line spacing)
- ○ check the design of a publication
- ○ save a template
- ○ make a copy of a template
- ○ use a template to create a variety of publications
- ○ set up a publication to print colour separations
- ○ set crop marks to print
- ○ print a template
- ○ print a composite copy
- ○ print colour separations.

If you think that you need more practice on any of the skills in the above list, go back and work through those skills again.

If you feel confident do the Build-up and Practice tasks on pages 65–76.

QUICK REFERENCE – *Creating a Master Page and template and displaying page content*

Keep a copy of this page next to you. Refer to it when working through tasks and during assessments.

HOW TO	METHOD
Close the Task Pane and start a new publication	Load Publisher → in the Task Pane, click the ✕ .
Display the Task Pane	Click on the View menu → click on Task Pane.
Set the Option to Close the Task Pane	Load Publisher → close the opening screen → click the Tools menu → click Options → check there is no tick in the box for Use New Publication task pane at startup.
Display the Master Page	Click on View → click on Master Page.
Create a non-standard page	Click on File → click on Page Setup → click on the Layout tab → in the Publication type section click on Custom → in the Width and Height boxes enter the required measurements → in the Orientation section click to select portrait or landscape.
Save a publication	Click on File → click Save As → click on the drop-down arrow to the right of the Save in box → locate your user area and open your working folder → in the File name box type the required filename → in the Save as type box, make sure Publisher Files is displayed → click the Save button.
Set margin and column guides	Click on Arrange → click on Layout Guides → in the Margin Guides section, enter the measurements for each of the margins → click on the Grid Guides tab → in the Columns box, enter the number of columns → click in the Preview pane → in the Spacing box enter the space between columns → click on OK.
Insert headers and footers	From the Master Page, click on View → click on Header and Footer → click on the Show Header/Footer icon 🖳 to switch between the header and footer → click on Format → click on Text Box then the Text Box tab → In the Text Box Margin section set all margins to 0 cm. *For headers* set the Vertical Alignment to Top. *For footers* set the Vertical alignment to Bottom. Click OK → click on the appropriate alignment icon and/or use the Tab key to select centre or right alignment → enter the text and/or click on the icon to enter the required information → click on Close .
Position ruler guides	Position the mouse on the appropriate ruler → click and drag the ruler guide to the required position → release the mouse button.
Remove ruler guides	Position the mouse on the ruler guide *in the margin area* of the publication → click and drag the ruler guide off the page → release the mouse button.

HOW TO	METHOD
Import (insert) an image	On the Objects toolbar click on the Picture Frame icon then Picture from File → move the mouse to the position where the image is to be placed → click and drag to draw a frame approximately the size you want the image to be → release the mouse button → locate and click on the image file to be inserted, then click Insert.
Resize an image maintaining proportion	Position your mouse on a CORNER handle of the image → click and drag the diagonal arrow inwards to make the image smaller or outwards to increase the size of an image → release the mouse button.
Resize an image to an exact size	Right-click on the picture → click on Format Picture → select the Size tab → check that there is a tick in the boxes for Lock aspect ratio and Relative to original picture size → in the Height or Width box enter the required measurement → click OK.
Move an image	Position your mouse on the image → click and drag the image to the required position then release the mouse button → take care NOT to drag on any of the corner or side handles of the image, or you will distort the original image.
Layer page items	Click on item to be layered → right-click on the item → click on Order → click on the required option.
Turn off hyphenation	Click on Tools → select Options → click on the Edit tab → in the box next to Automatically hyphenate in new text boxes, click to remove the tick → click on OK.
Create a text box	From the Objects Toolbar click the Text Box icon → click and drag the mouse to draw a text area to the required size → release the mouse button → if required, use the handles of the text frame to fit it exactly to the page layout guides. *After drawing the first text box in a publication* Click on Format → click on Text Box → click on the Text Box tab → set the Vertical Alignment (usually Top) → set Text Box Margins to 0 cm all round → check that Text auto-fitting is set to Do not autofit → click on the Colours and Lines tab → click Apply settings to new text boxes → click on OK.
Insert pages	Click on Insert → Click on Page → in the box next to Number of new pages enter the number of pages to be inserted → click to select Before current page or After current page → select Duplicate all objects on page or Insert blank pages → click on OK → use the page navigation buttons to move between the pages.
Delete pages	Ensure the page to be deleted is displayed on the screen → click on Edit → click on Delete page.
Import (insert) a text file and control text flow	Click in the text box where the text is to start → click on Insert → click on Text File and locate the file to be inserted → in the Files of type box, check that All Text Formats is displayed → click on the file to be inserted and click OK → if a File Conversion dialogue box displays check that the button for Windows (Default) is selected, then click OK → at the bottom of the first text box click on ⓐ⋯ → click on ⚭ → move your mouse into the text box where you wish the text to continue then click.

Unit 4: e-publication design

click means click with the left mouse button

QUICK REFERENCE – *Creating and applying style sheets and editing publications*

Keep a copy of this page next to you. Refer to it when working through tasks and during assessments.

HOW TO	METHOD
Remove styles	Click on **Format** → click on **Styles and Formatting** → click on the drop-down arrow next to the **Show** box, and select **All Styles** → hover over the bottom style and click on the drop-down arrow → click on **Delete** → click **Yes**.
Create new styles	Click on **Format** → click on **Styles and Formatting** → click on **Create new style** → in **Enter new style name** enter the name of the style → click on the drop-down arrow under **Style for the following paragraph** and select **Normal** → click on **Font...** → select the font settings → **OK** → click on **Paragraph** → set **Indents and spacing** → set **Line and Paragraph Breaks** → **OK** → **OK**.
Find text	Click on **Edit** → click on **Find** → in the box under **Find what** enter in the phrase of the text to find → click on **Find Next**.
Apply styles to text	To apply the **body text** → ensure the **Styles and Formatting Task Pane** is displayed → click in the text to be formatted → press **Ctrl+A** to highlight all text → in the **Styles and Formatting Task Pane** click on the body text style to apply → click on the desktop area (the grey area around the publication).
	To apply the **subheading style** → click anywhere in the first subheading → in the **Styles and Formatting Task Pane** click on the subheading style to apply it → repeat for each subheading → click on the desktop area.
	To apply the **heading style** → click anywhere in the heading → in the **Styles and Formatting Task Pane** click on the heading style → click on the desktop area.
Amend/change a style	Display the **Styles and Formatting Task Pane** → hover over the style to be changed then click on the drop-down arrow → select **Modify** → click on **Font** and/or **Paragraph** and make the necessary changes → click on **OK**, then click **OK** again.
Insert bullets	Select the lines to be bulleted → on the **Formatting** toolbar, click on the **bullets** icon → check that the spacing above and below the bulleted text is correct.
Amend the spacing between bullets and the text (optional)	Select all lines of the bulleted text → on the **Ruler** click and hold on the **Indent Marker** to drag it to the required position → click away from the bullet text to deselect the bulleted text.

HOW TO	METHOD
Amend text	Locate the text that is to be amended → make the required amendment → check the spacing before and after the amendment.
Apply a dropped/raised capital	Click in the paragraph to which you want to apply a dropped/raised capital → click on Format → click on Drop Cap → select a style → if required click on the Custom Drop Cap tab → in the box next to Size of letters enter the number of lines high you wish the dropped capital to be → click on Apply → click on OK.
Rotate text	Click on the text box containing the text to be rotated → click on the drop-down arrow to the right of the Free Rotate icon ⟲ → select the required rotation → adjust the text box to fit the area for the rotated text.
Reverse text	Select the text to be reversed → click on the drop-down arrow to the right of the Font Color icon → from the drop-down menu click on the white square → on the Formatting Toolbar click on the drop-down arrow to the right of the Fill Color icon → from the drop-down menu click on the required contrasting colour.
Create WordArt	On the Objects toolbar click on the Insert WordArt icon → click on the required style then click on OK → enter the required text → select the font, size and emphasis if required → click on OK → move the text to the required position and resize if necessary.
Insert and format lines and arrows	On the Objects toolbar click on the Line or the Arrow icon → click and drag to draw the line/arrow to the required size → release the mouse button → ensure the line/arrow is selected → right-click on the line/arrow → click on Format AutoShape → select the required line settings (for arrows click on the Begin Style and/or End Style and select the required settings) → click on the Layout Tab → select the required Wrapping Style.
Insert and format boxes	On the Objects toolbar click on the Rectangle → move the mouse to the position where the top-left corner of the box is to be placed → click and drag to draw the box to the required size → release the mouse button → ensure the box is selected (handles will appear around the box) → position the mouse over the box then right-click → click on Format AutoShape → in the Colors tab select the required fill and line click on the Layout Tab → select the required Wrapping Style and, if necessary, the Wrap Text required.
Layer objects	Select the object, right-click → click on Order → select required order.
Group and ungroup objects	On the Objects toolbar click on the Select objects icon → click and drag to draw a box that includes all the items to be grouped → click on the Group Objects icon → to ungroup the items click on the Ungroup Objects icon.
Copy, paste and move grouped items	Select the grouped items → click on the Copy icon → click on the Paste icon → position the mouse on top of the copy of the grouped objects → click and drag the copy of the grouped objects to the required position → click on the desktop to deselect the copied items.

QUICK REFERENCE – Copyfitting and printing publications

Click means click with the left mouse button

HOW TO	METHOD
Adjust the leading (line-spacing)	Display the final text box of the publication on the screen → open the **Styles and Formatting Task Pane** and hover over the style to be changed → click on the drop-down arrow → click on **Modify** → click on **Paragraph** → click in the box at the end of **Between lines** and enter the required measurement → click on **OK**, then **OK** again → check your adjustment fills the publication → repeat if necessary.
Check the design of a publication	Click on **Tools** → click on **Design Checker** → in the **Design Checker Task Pane** look at the problems identified → if required, hover the mouse over the listed problem and click on the drop-down arrow that appears → select the option to **Fix** or to **Go to this Item** to fix the problem manually → repeat until all problems are fixed.
Save a template	Save the publication in the normal way → close the publication → from **My Computer**, locate the file that is to be used as a template → click on the file → click on **File** → click on **Properties** → click on the **General tab** → in the box next to **Attributes**, click to put a tick in the box to the left of **Read only**.
Copy a template	Save the publication in the normal way → close the publication → from **My Computer**, locate the file that is to be copied → click on the file → click on **Edit** → click on **Copy** → click on **Edit** → click on **Paste**.
Use a template to create a variety of publications	Open a copy of the template (either the read-only file or the copy of the original file) → check that page 1 of the publication is displayed on the screen → insert the content of the publication → **Design Check** the publication → click on **File** → click on **Save As** → save the publication in the normal way.
Set up a publication to print colour separations	Open the publication to be printed → click on **Tools** → click on **Commercial Printing Tools** → click on **Color Printing** → click on **Spot Colours** → click on **OK** → check that the inks shown under the **Inks** tab are the correct colours to be used in the publication (if not, cancel, amend the publication and repeat from the start) → click on **OK**.
Set crop marks to print	Open the publication to be printed → click on **File** → click on **Print** → click on the **Advanced Print Settings** button → click on the **Page Settings tab** → click on **Crop marks** to place a tick in the box → click on **OK**.
Print a template or publication	Open the template or publication to be printed → if you are printing colour separations ensure you have set up the publication for colour separations → click on **File** → click on **Print** → *if* the **Change Copies Per Sheet** button is displayed, click **Change Copies Per Sheet** → click on **Print one copy per sheet** → click on **OK** → click on **OK**.

HOW TO	METHOD
Print a composite copy	Click on the Advanced Print Settings button → click on the Separations tab → check that the Output is set to Composite RGB or Composite Greyscale (if not click on the drop-down arrow at the end of the box to select) then click on OK → in the Print Range section, click on All → click on OK.
Print colour separations	Open the Print dialogue box → click on the Advanced Print Settings button → click on the Separations tab → click in the drop-down arrow at the end of the Output box and click on Separations → click on the drop-down arrow at the end of the These plates and click on Used Inks Only → in the Print plate section, check that there is a tick in the box next to each colour to be printed → click on OK → in the Print Range section, click on All → click on OK.

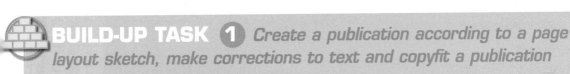

During the task you will need:

- the image file **rider**
- the image file **bike**
- the text file **diary**
- a printout of the Page Layout Sketch **T1LoutBU**
- a printout of corrections to text **T1TextBU**.

These files can be found in the subfolder **U4datafiles_buildtasks** on the CD-ROM supplied with this book.

1   Start Publisher and create a new publication. Format the document as follows:

Paper size:	**A4**
Orientation:	**Landscape**
Top Margin:	**15 mm (1.5 cm)**
Bottom Margin:	**15 mm (1.5 cm)**
Left Margin:	**10 mm (1 cm)**
Right Margin:	**10 mm (1 cm)**
Columns:	**3**
Space between columns:	**10 mm (1 cm)**

Remember to turn the hyphenation off.

2   Insert the following headers and footers:

	TEXT	ALIGNMENT
Header	your name and centre number	flush to left margin
Footer	automatic page number (starting at page 1)	centre
	Diary of a cyclist	flush to right margin

> **TIP!**
>
> Set the header and footer text box margins to 0 mm.

3   Set up the page layout as shown in the Page Layout Sketch (**T1LoutBU** provided on the CD-ROM).

4   Import text file **diary** and position it shown in the page layout sketch.

5   Import the image **rider** and position it at the bottom of column 2 on page 1 as shown on the Page Layout Sketch.

6   Place a thick border around this image.

7   Import the image **bike** and position it in column 2 of page 2 as shown in the Page Layout Sketch. Ensure that the image is visible behind the text.

8   Make the corrections shown in the document **T1TextBU** (provided on the CD-ROM).

9 Create a style sheet as follows:

body text:

style	**serif**
size	**10**
emphasis	**regular/normal**
alignment	**justified**

heading

style	**sans serif**
size	**24**
emphasis	**bold**
alignment	**centre**

subheading

style	**serif**
size	**14**
emphasis	**bold, italic**
alignment	**left**

10 Apply the body text style to the entire document.

11 Apply the heading style to the text: **Cycling for Charity**

12 Apply the subheadings style to the following 8 subheadings:

The Challenge
Day 1 London – Johannesburg
Day 2 Johannesburg – Prince Albert
Day 3 Prince Albert – Oudtshoorn
Day 4 Oudtshoorn – De Rust
Day 5 De Rust – De Hoop
Day 6 De Hoop – Knysna
Day 7 Knysna – Wilderness

13 Copyfit the publication ensuring that:

a The leading is adjusted so that there is no more than 10 mm (1 cm) of vertical white space anywhere in the document, except where indicated in the Page Layout Sketch.

b Columns are balanced to within 10 mm (1 cm).

c Leading is consistent.

d Paragraph spacing is consistent.

e There are no hyphenated line endings.

f Subheadings are kept with at least two lines of related text.

g There are no widows or orphans.

h All material is displayed as specified.

i The text file is displayed in full.

j Proportions of images are maintained.

14 Save the publication using the filename **trip**

15 Print a composite copy of the publication.

During the task you will need the image file **scene**.

Before you begin this task you will need to print the page layout sketch **T2LoutBU**.

These files can be found in the subfolder **U4datafiles_buildtasks** on the CD-ROM supplied with this book.

You have been asked to create a template that can be used to produce notices.

- You will need to prepare the template in two colours, **black** and **green**.
- You may use any fonts, sizes and styles for the text in this template, but you must only use the colours specified in the assignment.
- Refer to the page layout sketch for Build-up task 2 (provided on the CD-ROM) when competing this task.

1 Load Publisher.

2 Create a new publication using the measurements given in the Page Layout Sketch.

3 Use any margins and layout guides to suit your publication.

4 Draw a box with a solid black border to fill most of the height of your publication.

> **TIP!**
>
> For small publications choose small margins, e.g. 10 mm all round.

5 Position it on the left of your publication.

6 Make sure there is no fill to your box.

7 Create a text area/frame and enter the following text in **black** on two lines as shown:

Funds for Fun
a charitable organisation

8 Create a text area/frame and enter the following text in **green**:

Helping the Global

9 Create a text area/frame and enter the following text in **black** or **green**:
Community

10 Apply a special effect to this text.

11 Draw a thick black line above the text Helping the Global.

12 Draw a thick black line under the text Community.

13 Import the image **scene** and position it as shown.

14 The image will need to be re-sized but must be kept in proportion.

15 Save template using the filename **funds**

During the task you will need the image file **world**.

Before you begin this task you will need to print the page layout sketch **T3LoutBU**.

These files can be found in the subfolder **U4datafiles_buildtasks** on the CD-ROM supplied with this book.

You will also need the file **funds** that you saved in Build-up task 2.

1   Continue working on the file **funds** that you saved in Build-up task 2.

2   Group all the items in the publication.

3   Copy the grouped items and paste the **copy** on the right of the template as shown in the Page Layout Sketch.

4   Ungroup the **copy** of the grouped items.

5   Replace the image **scene** within the ungrouped items, with the image **world**.

6   The image will need to be re-sized but must be kept in proportion.

7   Insert your name and centre number as a header or footer.

8   Check your document to ensure you have followed all instructions.

9   Save this template, keeping the filename **funds**.

10 Set crop marks to print – check that only one copy will be printed per sheet.

11 Print a composite copy of the template showing crop marks.

12 Close the template.

BUILD-UP TASK ④ *Use a template to produce and print a colour-separated publication*

For this task you will need the following files:

○ **cyride** from the subfolder **U4datafiles_buildtasks**

○ **funds** that you saved in Build-up task 3.

1. Open a **copy** of the template **funds**.

2. Import the text file **cyride**.

3. Position this text in the white space in the centre of the publication.

4. **Centre** this text horizontally.

5. Colour this text **green**.

6. Display the text using fonts, styles and sizes to suit your publication.

7. Make sure that **all** the text is fully displayed and does not touch or overlap any page items.

8. Save your publication using the filename **newride**

9. Prepare colour-separated printouts.

10. Print a colour-separated copy of the publication.

11. Check that one print shows **only** the green items.

12. The colour of this printout must be shown on the print. You may need to handwrite the word '**green**' on this printout.

13. Check that one print shows **only** the black items.

14. The colour of this printout must be shown on the print. You may need to handwrite the word '**black**' on this printout.

15. Save your publication keeping the filename **newride.**

For this task you will need the following files:

- **volunt** from the subfolder **U4datafiles_buildtasks**
- **funds** that you saved in Build-up task 3.

1 Open a **copy** of the template **funds**.

2 Import the text file **volunt**.

3 Position this text in the white space in the centre of the publication.

4 Format the text using fonts, styles, sizes and alignment to suit your publication.

5 Make sure that **all** the text is fully displayed and does not touch or overlap any page items.

6 Save your publication using the filename **recruits**

7 Print a composite copy of your publication.

8 Close the file and exit Publisher.

Scenario

You are working as the Personal Assistant to the Manager of the Bemstead Community Centre. One of your jobs is to produce promotional materials for the Centre.

You will be required to produce a template and then use this to produce two flyers. You will also be required to produce a pamphlet that will be delivered to all houses in the area.

To produce the publications you will need the following files:

FILENAME	FILE TYPE
classes	text file
bandb	text file
community	text file
hall	image file
comp	image file
bricks	image file
books	image file
scout	image file

You will also need to refer to the Draft Documents on the CD-ROM provided with this book.

Before you begin any tasks you will need to print the following files:

- **PT1Lout** – the page layout sketch for Task 1.
- **PT2Lout** – the page layout sketch for Task 2.
- **PT5Lout** – the page layout sketch for Task 5.
- **PT5Text** – the text to be corrected in Task 5.

These files can be found in the subfolder **U4datafiles_practicetask1** on the CD-ROM supplied with this book.

You will need to use system software and application software that will allow you to:

- manipulate images
- combine text and graphics
- control page layout, columns and text flow
- print colour separated printouts.

TASK 1

Before you begin this task ensure you have printed:

○ the Page Layout Sketch for Task 1 (**PT1Lout**).

You will need the following files:

○ hall
○ comp

You have been asked to create a template that can be used to produce notices. The template will be used to produce two publications.

Unless specified, you may use any fonts, sizes and styles for the text in this template.

The Page Layout Sketch shows the approximate positioning of the text and images. Refer to the Page Layout Sketch for Task 1 when following all instructions for Task 1.

1   **a**   Using suitable software, create a new document template. Format the document as follows:

        Paper size: **A4**
        Orientation: **Portrait**

   b   Use any margins and layout guides to suit your publication.

2   **a**   Import the image **hall** and position it in the top-left of the document as shown.
   b   The image may be resized, but must be kept in proportion.

3   **a**   Create a text area/frame next to the image hall and enter the following text on one line as shown:

        Bemstead Village Hall

   b   Apply a special effect to this text (for example WordArt or reverse text).
   c   Make sure that the text does not touch or overlap any other page items.

4   **a**   Import the image **comp** and place it under the text keyed in at step 3.
   b   The image may be resized, but must be kept in proportion.

5   **a**   Draw a dashed line border around all the page items as shown in the layout sketch.
   b   Make sure there is no fill to your border and that the border does not touch or overlap any page items or extend into the margin space.

6   Save the template using the filename **bemstemp**

TASK 2

Before you begin this task ensure you have printed:

○ the Page Layout Sketch for Task 2 (**PT2Lout**)

You will need the following files:

○ the template **bemstead** (that you saved in Task 1)
○ **bricks**
○ **books**
○ **scout**

The Manager has requested some additions and changes to the template.

Refer to the Page Layout Sketch for Task 2 when following all instructions.

Continue working with the template **bemstead** that you saved in Task 1.

1 Group all the items in the publication.

2 Copy the grouped items and paste the **copy** at the bottom of the template as shown in the Page Layout Sketch.

3 Ungroup the **copy** of the grouped items.

4 Within the ungrouped items, delete the image **comp**.

5 Import the images **bricks, books** and **scout** and place them as shown in the Page Layout Sketch.

6 a Create a text area/frame and enter the following text on one line as shown:

   ACTIVITIES FOR ALL

   b Position this under the box at the top of the template as shown in the Page Layout Sketch.
   c Make sure that the text does not touch or overlap any other page items.

7 Insert your name and centre number as a header or footer.

8 a Check your document to ensure you have followed all instructions.
   b Save this template keeping the filename **bemstead**.

9 a Print a composite copy of the template.
   b Close the template.

PRACTICE TASK

TASK 3

Before you begin this task ensure you have the file **classes** and the template **bemstead** (that you saved in Task 2).

You have been asked to prepare a flyer advertising new courses.

1   Open a **copy** of the template **bemstead**.

2   a   Import the text file **classes**.
    b   Position this text in the white space in the centre of the publication.
    c   **Centre** this text horizontally.
    d   Display the text using fonts, styles and sizes to suit your publication.
    e   Make sure that **all** the text is fully displayed and does not touch or overlap any page items.

3   Save your publication using the filename **febclass**

4   a   Print a composite copy of your publication.
    b   Close the publication.

PRACTICE TASK

TASK 4

Before you begin this task ensure you have the file **bandb** and the template **bemstead** (that you saved in Task 2).

You have been asked to prepare a flyer to advertise the Friday bring and buy sales.

1   Open a **copy** of the template **bemstead**.

2   a   Import the text file **bandb**.
    b   Position this text in the white space in the centre of the publication.
    c   Format the text using fonts, styles, sizes and alignment to suit your publication.
    d   Make sure that **all** the text is fully displayed and does not touch or overlap any page items.

3   Save your publication using the filename **bringbuy**

4   a   Print a composite copy of your publication.
    b   Close the publication.

TASK 5

Before you begin this task ensure you have printed:

○ the Page Layout Sketch for Task 5 (PTLout)

○ the text to be corrected in Task 5 (PT5Text).

You will also need the file **community**.

You have been asked to prepare a two-page pamphlet about the activities held in the Community Centre. This will be a two-colour publication.

○ The text has been prepared for you.

○ You will be asked to make some amendments to this text.

○ The approximate positioning of the page items and text is shown on the Page Layout Sketch.

1 Create a new publication.

Format the document as follows:

Paper size	**As shown on the Page Layout Sketch**
Orientation	**Landscape**
All Margins	**10 mm (1 cm)**
Columns	**3 equal columns**
Space between columns	**10 mm (1 cm)**

2 Insert the following headers and footers:

	TEXT	ALIGNMENT
Header	**Bemstead Community Centre**	flush to right margin
Footer	your name and centre number	flush to left margin
	the date	flush to right margin

3 Set up the page layout as shown in the Page Layout Sketch for Task 5.

4 Import the text file **community** and position the text as shown in the Page Layout Sketch for Task 5.

Note: The text starts in column **3** of page **1**.

5 Make the corrections shown in the document Text to be corrected in Task 5.

6 **a** Format the **body text** to be:

style	**serif**
size	**9**
emphasis	**regular/normal**
alignment	**justified**
colour	**black**

b Format the heading **Bemstead CC** to be:

style	**sans serif**
size	**15**
emphasis	**bold**
alignment	**centre**
colour	**blue**

c Format the subheadings:

Classes
Sport
Children's Activities
Clinics
Outside Speakers
Trips
Can You Help?
to be:

style	**serif**
size	**12**
emphasis	**bold, italic**
alignment	**left**
colour	**blue**

7 Copyfit the publication ensuring that:

a The leading is adjusted so that there is no more than 10 mm (1cm) of vertical white space anywhere in the document, except where indicated in the Page Layout Sketch.
b Columns are balanced to within 10 mm (1cm).
c Leading is consistent.
d Paragraph spacing is consistent.
e There are no hyphenated line endings.
f Subheadings are kept with at least two lines of related text.
g There are no widows or orphans.
h All material is displayed as specified.
i The text file is displayed in full.

8 Save your publication using the filename **flybem**

9 Prepare colour-separated printouts.

a Set crop marks to print.
b Print a colour-separated copy of the publication.
c Check that one print shows **only** the blue items.
d The colour of this printout must be shown on the print. You may need to handwrite the word '**blue**' on this printout.
e Check that one print shows **only** the black items.
f The colour of this printout must be shown on the print. You may need to handwrite the word '**black**' on this printout.

10 a Save and close the publication keeping the filename **flybem**.
b Close any open documents and exit the application.

General assessment guidelines for all units

Before the assessment

You are advised to obtain a copy of the syllabus from the OCR website. Read through all the assessment objectives to ensure that you have the necessary skills before you begin an assessment.

Before you start a live assessment, complete at least two 'mock exams' in assessment conditions, without help from your tutor or classmates.

The assessment

- Level 2 assessments will usually be split into five or six tasks.
- You are allowed a notional duration of 3 hours for each assessment.
- Before you begin, read through the paper to see what you will need to do.
- You may want to allow yourself about 2½ hours to do all the tasks and then 30 minutes to check all your final printouts and your saved files.
- Your tutor may allow you to complete an assessment over several consecutive sessions (lessons).
- Once you start an assessment your tutor is not allowed to help you, so make sure that you are ready for the assessment before you start it.
- Your tutor will provide you with a photocopy of the original assignment.
- Printing can be done after the assessment, however, you are advised to print your work whenever there is an instruction to print.

> **TIP!**
>
> When you have printed your work, do not move straight onto the next instruction or task! Check your printout against the instructions in the assignment to make absolutely sure that you have carried out each instruction correctly and that the printout matches what you have on the screen.

During the assessment

During the assessment you are allowed to use the following:

- The Heinemann textbook that you worked through for your learning.
- The Quick reference guides from the Heinemann book.
- Your own notes.
- Handouts from your tutor that cover general IT skills.
- Any books that cover general IT skills.
- You are not allowed to use any books, notes, handouts etc. that are referenced to the assessment objectives of the syllabus.

- You cannot ask your tutor or anyone else for help.

- If there is a technical problem (e.g. something wrong with the computer or printer), then you should inform your tutor or the invigilator.

- Read through the whole task before you start.

- All the instructions are numbered, and many have sub-steps (a, b, c etc). Read through the whole step before you start doing anything.

- Follow each instruction in the correct sequence. Do not leave out an instruction intending to do it later.

- Tick each instruction when you have completed it.

- Check that you have completed a step fully and correctly before moving on to the next step.

- Don't rush!

- Enter all data in the same case as in the assignment.

- Enter all data as it is presented in the assignment, ignore any alternative spelling or grammar suggestions made by the software.

- Any data that you have to type in is presented in bold to help you see what you have to key in. You should not use bold emphasis unless you are told to do so in the assessment.

- Remember that if you find an error you can correct it, but if you leave the checking to your tutor, they cannot give your work back to you to correct any errors that they have found.

- If you notice an error, you can make changes to your work and print again.

- Remember that you can print as many draft copies as you wish, but you must remember to destroy any incorrect copies or unwanted drafts.

- You will be asked to enter your centre number, and can enter this in any format (e.g. Centre Number 11111, Centre No 11111, Centre 11111, 11111).

TIP!

Read through all the instructions for the task before you start. If you are required to save the file with a different filename then do so before you start the task. This way you will not save over a file for the previous task.

At the end of the assessment

- Check your printouts against the assessment paper. Use a differently coloured pen/pencil, to tick each instruction again in the assessment.

- Make sure that you have saved all your files and have saved with the correct filename.

- Make sure that all your files are saved in the correct user area and that every printout has your first and last name on it.

- Arrange your prints in the order of tasks in the assignment.

- Destroy any printouts that you do not wish to be marked (or hand these to your tutor, making sure that your tutor knows these are not to be marked!).

- Hand the following to your tutor:
  - your final printouts in the correct order, you may wish to staple these to keep them secure
  - the copy of the assessment paper
  - the disk where you have saved your files (if you save on disk), if not tell the tutor where your files are saved on the computer.

Assessment guidelines for Unit 4

- Your tutor will provide you with all the files you need for the assessment.
- Before an assessment you should create a new folder just for the assessment.

TIP!

Before you start, *COPY* the folder containing the files into another folder in case you need to open an original file again.

- You will usually be provided with three or four image files and three or four text files. Before you begin the tasks, open the text files to familiarise yourself with the content so that you can be sure that you have imported all the text correctly. You are advised to print these files as an aid to checking that the text all has been imported into your publications.
- The order of tasks will vary from paper to paper. You will usually need to create one template, which you will use to produce several publications and one publication consisting of several pages. In one publication you will need to produce colour separated printouts. At least one publication will use a non-standard page size and you will need to print crop-marks on at least one small publication.

During the assessment, you will need to complete about five or six tasks

General assessment tips

- Follow each instruction in the correct sequence. Do not leave an instruction intending to do it later.
- Do not enter any text in bold unless instructed. The text is presented in bold to help you to identify filenames, text to be entered and instructions.
- If asked to insert page numbers do not type the page number; you must use the automatic page number facility on the master page of your publication.
- Save your work frequently. This is especially important for larger publications.
- Turn hyphenation off as soon as you open a new publication.
- After inserting the first text box in a publication format the text box margins to be 0 cm all round and apply these settings to all new text boxes.
- When producing smaller publications ensure that you set the print option to print only one copy per page (this is very important when crop marks are required).

- When producing a two-colour publication ensure you use **only** the two colours specified (or a shade of those two colours).
- If a special text effect has been used on a two colour publication, ensure that the special text effect does not use any other colours.
- If your printer is not able to print colour separations you **MUST** submit:
  - a screen print from the advanced print settings, separations window showing that the correct settings have been applied
  - a composite printout of the publication.
- Make sure you save each publication using the correct filename at the point that you are instructed to save. This is especially important if your work is to be assessed electronically (e.g. e-portfolio).
- You are advised to enter filenames using the same case as in the assignment. However, you will not be penalised if you use different case for filenames. Do not enter a full stop after a filename.
- Headers and footers must be entered on the master page. Unless there is a specific instruction, you may use any font size, font type and alignment for headers and footers. A small font size (between 8 and 10) is usually best.
- You will be asked to enter your name; it is good practice to enter your first and last name.

Template

There will usually be two tasks relating to the creation of a template. You will need to:
- set the page size and orientation
- place page items according to a page layout sketch
- insert headers and footers.

You may need to:
- set margins
- import/insert text and/or images
- resize text and images to suit your publication
- layer text and images
- use special text effects
- insert and format lines and boxes
- group page items
- copy paste and move grouped items
- amend page content
- print colour separations
- print a composite copy of the template.

Note that the papers will vary, so the above will not always be tested in the template, some of these skills may be tested in the two-page publication.

Template assessment tips

- Place **all** template items on the master page.
- You may be given a choice of font type, size and alignment for some or all of the text, however, you must ensure that all text is clearly visible on the page (do not use sizes smaller than 8pt).
- Pay particular attention to ensure last word of text in each text box is displayed in full.
- Check that page items do not touch or overlap (unless specified in instructions and/or the Page Layout Sketch).
- Use the 'zoom' facility to check the layout of page items.
- When borders are applied to a text box, you may need to adjust the text box margins to prevent the text from touching the border of the box (a margin of 0.1 cm is usually sufficient).
- When layering items check that all items have been layered as specified and that any text can still be read.
- When grouping items ensure that **all** specified items have been grouped.
- Check that you have followed the Page Layout Sketch.
- Ensure that all images are in proportion.
- Ensure all items are placed within the page margins.
- Run the 'Design Checker' to help identify any problems, and make any necessary corrections.
- Check your work very carefully to ensure that you have not made any errors.
- Ensure that you save the template with the specified filename.
- Set the properties of the completed template to be read-only and make a copy of the template.

Creating publications using a template

There will usually be two tasks.

- You will generally need to:
    - use the template that you created to produce two different publications
    - import a text file and/or image(s) into the publication
    - follow instructions on where to place text and or images in at least one publication
    - display the text and images to suit your publication in at least one publication
    - instructed to save the publication using a specified filename.

Creating publications using a template assessment tips

- Make sure you place page items on Page 1 of the publication (not the Master Page).
- Ensure that text and graphics do not overlap any items on the Master Page.

- You may be given some instructions on how to display the text (e.g. colour and centre) but will usually be given a choice of font type and size for some or all of the text. You must ensure that all text is clearly visible on the page (do not use sizes smaller than 8pt).

- Check your work carefully to ensure that you have followed all instructions.

- Pay particular attention to ensure that the last word of text (and associated punctuation) is displayed in full.

- Check that all items are displayed within the page margins and do not touch or overlap (unless specified).

- Run the 'Design Checker' to help identify any problems, and make any necessary corrections.

Creating a multi-page publication

There will usually be one task. You will need to:

- create a new page layout for a publication
- set the publication size, orientation, margins, columns and space between columns
- set and apply layout guides following page layout sketches and text flow diagrams
- import text file(s) and may also need to import image(s) into the publication
- enter headers and footers
- make correction to text according to proof correction symbols
- apply styles to text (usually three different styles)
- copyfit and check the publication
- save the publication using a specified filename.

Creating a multi-page publication assessment tips

- Turn off hyphenation as soon as you create the new publication.
- Enter headers and footers on the master page.
- Switch to normal view before inserting any page items.
- Check the Page Layout Sketches very carefully – remember the text will not always start on page 1 or in column 1!
- Use rulers to help you position page items.
- Remove all existing styles in the style sheet before creating new styles.
- For **body text** tick **widow and orphan control**.
- For **subheadings** tick **keep with next**.
- Unless otherwise specified, you may use paragraph space (between 3pt and 6pt is usually sufficient) for body text, subheadings and headings. Choose space before or after paragraphs but *not* both!).
- You may use a first line indent for body text, however, it is not advisable to use a first line indent with dropped capitals or with a paragraph space.

- After making corrections to the text, check the spacing before and after the amendment very carefully.
- Remember that there should be only one space after a full stop and only one hard return (enter press) at the end of a paragraph.
- When copyfitting the publication:
  - check that all styles have been applied to the text before starting the copyfitting process
  - remember that 'white space' includes shaded and/or solid areas that are not broken by a line, image or text
  - ensure you are on the final page of the publication and can see the final words of text
  - always amend the line spacing through modifying the body text in the style sheet
  - adjust the line spacing in small increments (remember that you can key in numbers with up to three decimal places e.g. 1.112) – try making small amendments first to see the effect
  - remember that you can adjust images and/or empty/blank areas to assist in the copyfitting process – you must, however, ensure that images are kept in proportion
  - unless specified images do not need to fit the entire width of the column there may be horizontal white space either side of images (but not more than 10 mm of white space above or below the image – unless specified in the design brief)
  - hyphenation, widows and orphans and subheadings split from related text should have been controlled through the style sheet – but it is still advisable to do a visual check of the top and bottom of each column
  - after copyfitting check that the final words in the publication are still displayed.
- Run the 'Design Checker' to help identify any problems, and make any necessary corrections.

Check all printouts for accuracy.

Good luck!

Index